GO PLAY
IN THE SAND,
JOHN

John Tipping
with Frances Kavanagh

First published in Great Britain in 2008
By KavanaghTipping Publishing
Wingham Business Centre, Goodnestone Rd,
Wingham CT3 1AR

With thanks to Ben and Abby Cohen for permission
to include their photograph.
Photograph of John and Jill, 'Behind every good
man ...' by DJE Photographic.

For Jilly,
for all the years
she's put up with me.

CONTENTS

PICTURE GALLERY

FOREWORD

Go Play in the Sand, John is a contradiction and an irony: a memoir by a severely dyslexic man who can neither read nor write and will probably never be able to read his own book.

For it to become a reality, the book obviously had to be written by someone else – me, the ghost writer – whose input is generally far from the reader's radar. However, John asked me to write a foreword after I commented that if I were in research I would have his head covered in electrodes to watch his brain in action. In reality, I have no idea whether electrodes are even used in the observation of the brain; the comment was more an expression of my level of interest.

Dyslexia is a term that many have heard but few really understand. It is a complex condition of the brain that affects some or all of the development of skills connected with language and literacy, and manifests as learning difficulties. John's dyslexia, being extremely severe, accurately reflects the root meaning of the word, which has its etymological origins in Greek: 'dus', meaning bad or difficult, and 'lexis', meaning speech. John's early speech development was affected, as well as his ability to learn to read and write.

The condition is not connected to intelligence, or lack thereof. Many dyslexic people demonstrate higher intelligence than the norm and they are often more insightful, creative and intuitive than average, with unusual perceptual abilities. They have a different kind of mental acumen more inclined to lateral thinking, or thinking 'outside the box'. It is a more visceral connection with the unconscious, resulting in ideas and inspiration that logic alone does not produce.

From this perspective, people with dyslexia (and associated disorders, such as attention deficit hyperactivity disorder – ADHD - and attention deficit disorder - ADD) may be demonstrating significantly different thinking processes imbued with as much, if not more, achievement potential as the norm. The present focus, however, is on *disorder*, as an impediment to learning, not on *difference* and the intrinsic value of heightened creative thinking processes that may require fundamentally diverse teaching approaches. At the rate they are occurring, dyslexia and associated disorders are a phenomenon that would benefit from as broad a perspective as possible because, without a doubt, there is still much to be learned *from* them, as well as about them.

Research presently focused on the cerebellum offers hope of more effective solutions to the difficulties, frustration and suffering of those affected by these conditions. The Dore Programme (www. dore.co.uk), to which John refers, is a system of physical and mental exercises that focuses on the functioning of the cerebellum. It is expensive and therefore not readily accessible to many who would benefit from it, and it is not the answer for everyone, but it does indicate that natural procedures based on neurological findings are possible.

In order to provide as much insight as possible into the workings and life consequences of a deeply dyslexic brain, John spoke this book into existence. It is written in his inimitable 'voice', which helps communicate the profoundly frustrating and disabling aspect of his condition: that of an intelligent mind hindered by an under-functioning brain. The way John expresses himself is one demonstration of his continual endeavour to make his brain function to requirements and facilitate his intelligence: it reflects the dyslexia that partly defines him.

Contributions from John's family, while adding perspective to events, also stand like low relief sculpture, elucidating, to some extent, the differences between his everyday thinking and speaking performance and the norm, giving an overall impression of John pushing his intellect through channels too narrow to accommodate it.

He has an intriguing, almost objective awareness, undoubtedly born of necessity, of his brain activity. The usual experience of the brain is in conjunction with the mind, many believing they are one and the same. We do not consciously experience brain function any more than we consciously experience liver, heart, or any other autonomic organ function, unless it is through pain. We *use* the brain, but we do not generally have sufficient detachment to delineate how we normally experience it, nor do we have a direct and interactive relationship with it, as it would appear John does, at some level. He is much more conscious of it as separate from the person he is – his essential being-ness. On occasion, when trying to remember something, he would address his brain directly, saying, 'Come on, brain, drag it out!'

Fundamentally, John's story might be described as a modern myth or fairy tale, as it contains elements of both: the seemingly impossible tasks; the measured help in various guises at critical moments, and the tests of endurance before winning the hand of a queen and a realm of opportunity over which he has dominion. Those elements, aided by John's insight, produce a story of metamorphosis, emergence and hope that has universal relevance.

Years of speech therapy enabled John to develop verbal skills. There was nothing similar when it came to literacy. He learned the power of the written word the hard way: by being deprived of it. Now, with passionate determination, he is using it to inspire others, to communicate a deeper understanding of dyslexia to educators and parents, and to raise the awareness of the general public. Despite all the obstacles, he articulates a complexity of emotion and experience with moving clarity.

Frances Kavanagh

PREFACE

The main drive behind this book is to show that an ordinary guy, like me, can change his attitude through his own will to change. It's for people who have lived for years knowing they want to better themselves. That's what we all want – to better ourselves – whether it's financially, or how you feel just getting up in the morning. We can do that. All the tools we need to do it are in us. We get help but, at the end of the day, we do it ourselves.

Some people might wonder what I mean by 'tools': they're techniques you can use to live your life. My tool bag is full of my confidence, which I carry about with me. Self-worth is the key one for me; finding it was everything. I'm severely dyslexic, so I'm different in the way I think because of the way my brain is set up, but still I'm no different than anybody else: I can give.

I would love to be a champion for other dyslexic people and help to move them on. I can only give my story; it will be the person who moves him or herself on. Yes, you get help, but it's only you who can do it, nobody else. I had an experience that was like being born again, and it may sound 'wimpy' but I still have moments like that every so often. I fill up even now because I'm amazed that it has changed so much for me.

Even though I've got a hidden disability, I've got myself further in my career, in my business, in my life than anybody thought I would, including me. I could have done that working for somebody, but I never found the person who understood and accepted me, and helped move me on. I went out on my own to do that in business.

The book is directed at everybody. It is mainly people who have dyslexia who will relate to me, but we all have our demons holding us back frozen by fear of what will happen. Most of the time, what we fear doesn't happen. It's the thought of it that stops us from acting. If it does happen, we can usually cope with it; we're more grown up than we think we are!

It's a *weird* feeling – absolutely bizarre - to have my autobiography out, because I've never read a book in my life, and it would be quite ironic if I were to do any book signings. I could sign my name, but the customer would have to write the message!

I just want the chance to touch other people's lives. It would be brilliant if hearing what I've been through, and still have to get over every day to make me grow as a human being, helps them a little bit to create their full potential.

As humans we talk rubbish eighty percent of the time. The odd twenty percent, we talk sense, and we all know that's true. Maybe the people who read this only need to read twenty percent of it - but they'll have to read all of it to find the twenty percent!

What I hope to get across is that if I can do it, anybody can. We can have the life we want. We can find the way to do it.

PART ONE

THE PIT

MY DYSLEXIA

I'm forty-two years old. Until I was thirty-seven I just existed. Then I really started living my life, so I'm actually only five years old! They say life begins at forty; I started three years early!

Five years ago, I woke up. I became me. Everything came alive. Some people would say I lost thirty-seven years of my life by just existing, but I've got lots more years ahead of me, and I'm awake and enjoying it all.

For thirty-seven years, confidence was non-existent for me; I didn't know what it was. I heard all those words – confidence, self-worth, self-esteem, and so on - but they meant nothing to me. I didn't even realise I didn't have self-worth or self-esteem. At the same time, there was something in the back of my mind saying, *don't give up; one day it will get better*, even though I had no idea how it could be. I didn't get dealt the best hand in life, and it still does, on occasion, feel like everybody got the aces, and I got left with the crap cards. When I was thirty-seven, though, I was dealt a new load of cards and got quite a few aces. I wouldn't have said this five years ago, but, ironically, even with all the depression I've had over the years because of my dyslexia – and there was no other reason for my depression, but dyslexia – I wouldn't swap it. Without dyslexia, I wouldn't be me.

I have an amazing life. One of my ambitions is to live to a grand old age, and my vision of dying is being on my deathbed with everybody around me who I love, and I can look back and go, 'Wow! That was a really beautiful life.' I don't think many people can say that on their deathbed. If it happened tomorrow, I could say that now.

I've got one of the worst kinds of dyslexia anyone can have: it's actually total. It's very unusual, and I've only ever met one other guy who's as dyslexic as I am – that's one other person in over forty years. There are so many different levels of dyslexia and they're not all the same. There are similarities but everyone is slightly different, so what works for one person doesn't work for another, and that's what makes it so difficult for the experts to be able to teach everyone to read and write. That can knock a dyslexic person's confidence to the floor, and you're frozen with fear, with no competence to be able to do much about it. Some dyslexics work out a muddled system of their own that works for them, because we have to create our own way of dealing with the world that is completely different to normal people. There may be a magic cure out there somewhere; miracles happen everyday, and I fully believe that, but it's finding it. The cerebellum seems to be the key and that can be trained.

When I was a kid, other dyslexics could either read or write but struggled with both. With mine, from the time I can remember, I struggled with everything, including getting my words out. I didn't start talking until I was three, and then I had a speech impediment, which they had to work on until I was eight or nine to get me talking properly. No one knew about dyslexia then, and they kept on saying that I got behind in my schooling because I had to work so hard on my speech. I wasn't diagnosed with dyslexia until I was fourteen.

We didn't have a car until I was about twelve, so we had to get a train over from Broadstairs to Margate to go to the speech therapist. I don't remember much about any of it. If I sat down and really, really tried, maybe I could, but those memories would be quite painful. The one thing I do remember is the speech therapist saying, 'Go and play in the sand, John.' By all accounts, I tried so hard to get words out that I clenched my fists. The speech therapist didn't notice to begin with and then, one time, she saw there was blood running down my hands. I had dug my fingernails in, and I was concentrating so much that I hadn't realised it. Once it had happened, she'd notice when my knuckles were going almost white, and she'd tell me to go and play in the sand, to make me relax and do something I liked.

My brain does not work in the normal way (if there is a normal way): I have to select information coming at me more consciously than the average person, and I've had to train my brain over the years, just to cope with everyday life. When someone talks to me, the words have to go in, then my brain processes them, and then I can respond. For most people that's fairly instant; for me, it takes a few moments. The way I think is not so bad now because I'm more confident, and I know I can deal with it better. I stay calm; whereas, in the past, I was anxious all the time because I was so worried I was going to look stupid; that was the constant fear that lived with me all the time. Now, if somebody is talking to me too fast, I'll ask them to slow down or give me a few moments to get what they're saying, or I ask them to repeat it. If I move myself away from me, I can see why I was called 'slow'. I've conditioned my brain to be able to cope, but if somebody talks fast, I still really struggle to get the information in. I recognize the individual words, but there's too much information coming at me all at once, so my brain takes more time to make out the sentence. I do, and lots of dyslexic people do *have* to take their time to get the information programmed into their brain to be able to give back the answer. It's the same with everything and, like a computer, if too much information comes in it can crash. I have to re-live or re-route everything in my brain to be able to deal with everyday information and living.

I would say that, in some ways, dyslexia is almost like dementia; I really would. When I get old, if I get senile, no one is going to tell any difference because I won't seem to be any different at all. It's the only way I can say what it's like. People with dementia go off into other worlds, forget things, forget what they're saying. That happens to me. Quite often, if I'm in a business meeting – I dread them; you can train yourself to get over that but it takes a long time - I'm half way through a sentence, and they might be listening really intently, and the next word is suddenly completely gone, so it seems like I'm not very intelligent. It's pressure, because, at the end of the day, we're talking about money, which you have to earn to survive, and a bad business meeting can lose you thousands of pounds where it could have earned you thousands of pounds.

I have what I call 'dyslexic days', when nothing is clear. At the end of those days, I have complete and utter mental exhaustion just from doing the basic things. Most people can get a sentence out with no trouble. I have to use my brain ten, twenty, thirty, one hundred times more and concentrate harder to get that same sentence out.

It's like somebody being picked up from this country and put down in the middle of China: they have never spoken Chinese in their life, but they're expected to talk Chinese straight away, go out and work, make a living, have a family and so on. They would be just so far out of their comfort zone they wouldn't know what to do. That's what dyslexia is like for me, and it must be the same for lots of other dyslexic people: as soon as you walk out the door, you're out of your comfort zone and you have to push yourself every day. Sometimes the English language is *so* difficult and an awful lot is learned or picked up about that, and everything in life, from reading. I've had to learn what I can from visual clues and listening to people.

Small things can really throw you and you can panic, like whenever I go on a work site I have to sign in, and no signing in book is ever the same, so you can't familiarise yourself with them. Things like that can happen at any given moment in the day, and you don't know when or how many there might be. I might be driving down a road I've driven down thousands of times and I have to turn right in a minute and, all of a sudden, I completely forget which way I have to go. I'm not far away from that junction, and I just cannot think which way I have to turn, or where I go after I turn. I'm coming up to that junction, and if I'm not careful panic sets in. That happens to me on a daily basis and I used to be very, very panicky, but I have to believe it will come back to me, and most of the time it does now.

Last year, I tiled the bathroom and it came out quite well; I was quite pleased about it. I'd never done tiling in my life. But now, eighteen months later, I cannot remember how to tile. It's completely gone because my brain has to get rid of a lot of information to do the normal everyday things. My thought patterns take slightly longer to get round because of my dyslexia: it's the way my brain is set up. It's like you want to go to London from the south coast: you can go more or less straight there on the motorway; for me, it's like going via Liverpool - it takes ten times longer. It's hard work for the brain. It's all there somewhere - everything I've learned over forty-two years – but, with dyslexia, you have to make such a total effort to drag it out and remember, everything is so much slower.

I understand that now, because I've had forty-two years of working it out, and I'm an adult. Working it out in my earlier life, especially when I was a kid, was like hitting my head against a wall, constantly, every way I turned. It's like when you're a kid and you put your hand near a flame: before you burn yourself, most of the time, someone will tell you it will hurt. It's like doing that constantly in every circumstance, but nobody's telling you it will hurt: you're learning something and you find it's too difficult, so you have to find another way.

It's just hard work. There have been times, even in the last year, when I've woken up and had to really, really think what my name is. You just cannot think what your name is. You know you're you, and you know you know your name, but you just cannot think of it. It's actually quite scary, waking up and not knowing your own name. With other people, even now, I very seldom use names because I cannot remember names at all. On the odd occasion, I have to think what Jill's name is, or the kids' names. I've had days like that trying to think what village I live in, and it just will not come.

It's not so much now, because I have a very weird system that my brain runs to; it knows it works that way. I'm not even aware of what the system is; my brain has found it, and those bad dyslexic days are very few now. I go into the system more naturally now, but I'd say I was in my mid-thirties before I really started, subconsciously, using that strange system in my brain.

My brain confuses me on a regular basis: it likes putting its foot out and tripping me up. It has a mind of its own! In my experience with me – I'm saying it that way for a reason - I would say the mind and the brain are two different entities that, for years, have been fighting against one another, and we're trying to find ways of working together.

I'm very visual and I don't have sounds in my head. I don't know about other dyslexics, but I don't have the sounds of words going through my mind. I could live to be a hundred and practice every day, and there's no way I could learn to read the traditional phonics way – learning with sounds. I would improve a little bit, but sometimes the amount of effort you have to put in to get one inch further on would just take up the whole of your life and, like everybody, we have to make money to survive. I would be able to say what a letter is – the name of the letter – but to sound it out, I really, really struggle. I might get single letters, but when they start stacking up together to make a word I can't do it. My brain recognises *something:* I can look at the word 'fox' and I want to say 'wolf', but I know it's not 'wolf'. One time, I was looking at the word 'cottage', and I knew it was a little house. I could have spelt out the letters of 'cottage', but I just couldn't remember what it was. It might come to me all of a sudden, or it won't.

At the moment, most reading, for me, would have to be connected with memory – memorising words. Experts would say put an association with the words, but that doesn't work for me because I'd have to associate so many different things with so many different words. I've had people say, 'Is it because, deep down, you don't want to read and write?' But *I can't do it.* Someone could tell me a word or I could sound it out, but then five or ten minutes later, it's completely gone. Even with endless repetition, it doesn't stay with me; by the time I get to the end of a sentence, I've forgotten what's at the beginning.

I think in pictures. I never see a word in my head, at all, and I struggle to see a letter in my head, so if somebody is spelling a word out for me it's very, very slow for me to get it down. Some days I'm better at it than others, but I have to concentrate really hard to pull the letters out of my brain. There are particular sounds that are more difficult than others: 'm' and 'n', for instance, are very difficult, and I get 's' and 'c' mixed up or can't remember them at all. I might have to say the letter over and over, and then what it looks like will come to me.

You could show me a line or a page of writing and I could tell you what all the letters are, and I could tell you some of the sounds, but then, half way down the page, a sound I've just given for a letter minutes before will be completely gone. Or, I could possibly sound out a word and then - the same word a little way down the page - I might be able to sound it out again, or not at all. I could spell it out, but not read it. I can name every letter, and people have said to me, 'But you just spelt it out. Why can't you read it?' Because I can't!

I know I have to be taught in a different way. Some people do juggling and train their brain. I'll get the money, one day, and I will do it. I think it might help me, though I'll be very surprised if it completely cures me, but it might trigger something off in my brain. You don't know until you try. If that doesn't work I can't see anything else working.

It definitely wouldn't work sitting down day after day with somebody, learning the old fashioned way, which works for most people. It's the sound that's the stumbling block, and it's the most frustrating thing imaginable when you've been told a word ten, twenty, a thousand times before, and on occasion sounded it out, and seconds, minutes, days, weeks or months later, it's completely *gone*. Nothing there! The teacher might say, 'You read that thirty seconds ago!' Yes, I remember doing it, but I don't remember what it is!

Every day, just looking at the written word is going out of my comfort zone. There were times when I would physically come out in a cold sweat at the sight of it or having to write something down. Years ago, if you went in to pay for anything, it was either cash or cheque. I've never carried a lot of cash; it's always been a chequebook, and I used to love it when the people had a stamp for who it was payable to. That's why I think cards and pin numbers are brilliant. Even remembering the number at one time was difficult, but I've trained myself to remember.

I've been quite lucky: I don't find numbers too difficult, although my maths isn't that brilliant; there was more concentration in school on trying to improve my English and the maths side of it was missed. I do have dyslexia with figures on occasion, though: somebody will give me a telephone number and I'll write it down wrong, miss numbers or press the wrong buttons. I hear what they say and put down a different number, or I put them the wrong way round. Same as words, I hear everything that's said, I just can't process it quickly enough. The brain doesn't filter anything like that out; it just takes it via Australia! When the brain is so involved with sorting it out, I have to wait a moment. If I can't process the information enough, I will ask again.

At one time I wouldn't write a cheque. Jill or my first wife would do it, or, if I were on my own, I'd have to ask the people there to write it for me. I still do on the odd occasion. 'Twenty' is an awful number for me to write, and 'thirty', a bit, as well, because everything I write is solely from memory. I'm not so bad with the other numbers. Those are the two main ones, although I struggle with 'hundred' as well.

I've never tried to hide the fact that I can't read or write. I am so severely dyslexic I just have to say if there is a problem, rather than trying to cover it up and just looking stupid.

I can only learn new vocabulary by hearing it and I constantly used to use words wrongly - I'd get the meaning wrong in embarrassing ways. I once told someone I had no kinetic ability, instead of phonetic, and then wondered why I got a weird look. I still do, sometimes: I hear a word slightly wrong, or say it out of context. It's the same as children picking up words before they can read. A classic one was 'City & Guilds': I thought it was 'Sitting Guilds', and 'ends meet', I thought, was 'hens meet'. We do quite often roll our words together, and if someone doesn't separate their words clearly, I get it wrong. For years I said 'igorant' instead of 'ignorant' because that's the way I heard it, and because I said it in that way, I was ignorant! Now I'm slightly deaf, as well, because of working on the roads with loads of different noises, so I have to be very careful that I hear things right, and I often ask people to repeat questions. That makes you look even slower. I wouldn't have used half the words I use, now, five years ago, because I didn't have the confidence in saying them; I thought I'd get them wrong. I still do get words out of context – it's part of my dyslexia – but I just accept that now.

Like most men, I really can only do one thing at a time, but I have trouble concentrating even on one thing, because I have to use a lot of brainpower to do it. Jill, my wife, finds that very frustrating because I get that glazed look. I think a lot of men do that, but I find it very easy to just clear my brain and I can keep it blank. Then, it's almost like rebooting a computer, and sometimes it's really difficult to get it going again. Every morning, I still have to make a conscious effort to think what day it is. Jill helps me out so much. It's very hard work and tiring living with somebody with my degree of dyslexia. She's always just accepted it, though. She's the first person in my life who really accepted me with my disability. She just lets me be me.

My brain has compensated to get me through life, but it could be so much better. Lots of people say that I have a kind of wisdom or perceptiveness, maybe it's intuition, and I think you develop that because, in some sense, there's part of my brain that I can't use at all, so what I *can* use has to be heightened, in the same way that a blind person's hearing is highly sensitive. You have to use what you've got.

When I was a kid it was more subconscious, like something telling me something at the back of my brain. From being a little kid, I knew something was wrong and different. People said I was slow and stupid but, deep down, I knew I wasn't. It was such a *relief* when I got diagnosed with dyslexia, because I had a name for what was wrong. In some ways it was the best thing to happen, but in so many *more* ways it was the worst: I had a label stuck right across my forehead, saying, *I am dyslexic so I cannot do life.* Simple as that, and that label can mean so many different things to so many different people, depending on the individual problem that they've got. Until you rip that label off and know that you're different in a positive way, you just exist. I'm living proof of that.

When I was a kid, adults told me I was stupid and I believed them. Up until I was thirty-seven, I would look in the mirror and hate myself because I was dyslexic. But deep, deep down, right at the very back of my brain something was saying, *you'll show them, one day, that they are wrong.*

I was told by an uncle or some other adult – I can't remember exactly who - that we were working class, and working class people don't run their own businesses; what you 'had down' was all you'd have for the rest of your life. When I heard that, in some way I thought, *I will run my own business one day.* I didn't know what it would be and, with my dyslexia, I knew I'd have to work for somebody but, looking back, I just didn't believe what he said. I just knew that you could better yourself somehow. I was about twelve at the time, so that would be 1977, when it was unheard of to be able to better yourself. Two or three years before that was the three day week; it was a crap time, and everything even looked dowdy. It's different now: there's more money, more choice.

I didn't *think* I was capable of more; it was just a feeling I had, from almost as long as I can remember, that there was more I could give and, someday, I'd have my own business. I wouldn't have said it, but I felt different from the working class way of thinking. It was a 'double whammy' – being dyslexic and working class - because there was something telling me somewhere that you *can* do it, and so many people saying you can't, so you think you must be wrong. For some reason, people always believe the bad parts and what they think they *can't* do is true. Most of the time that's a load of cobblers – a real load of crap – and if I can make one person with dyslexia believe that, then it's worth all the trouble I've gone through and still have to go through on a daily basis. There are loads of people who can excel beyond their wildest dreams. They just don't do it because they think they can't. The key to everything is self-belief.

Another of the compensating abilities for my dyslexia is being able to step back, and it's done me a lot of good. I think it was built in so that I could slow the world down and get off for a few moments. If I hadn't been able to do that instinctively, I wouldn't have been able to cope with what the world had to throw at me. Something at the back of my mind gave me the tools to be able to do that. Without it, I would have ended up in a lunatic asylum. I've done it so much over the years - whenever there was something new being thrown at me - and I do it in daily life quite often. In a normal conversation, for instance, I have to step back for a moment and think about the information that's coming at me.

I think if you keep calm, most things are instinctive. It's just having the confidence to take the time and not panic. A typical example:

five days before Christmas I was going out to a meeting, I was driving along just round the corner from where I live, and a girl walked out from behind a bus. I was doing about twenty miles per hour and I hit her. The sound of the impact was just like a cannon going off, and she was rocketed across to the other side of the road. Automatically, I instantly stopped the van. She went to get up and, in case she'd broken something, I told her, 'Stay where you are! Give yourself a moment!' That was instinctive for me. I was talking to the policeman afterwards, and he said that it's usually the 'fight or flight' instinct that kicks in and causes people to react in a completely different way, so that some people would have put their foot down and gone. Hit and run happens.

For me, being in the habit of putting the brake on the world, getting off and then getting back on after I've had a chance to think for a moment, made me react the way I did. I think it's built into all of us to be able to step back, and it only takes a moment. It's being open to thought instead of reacting straight away. It does make a difference: you see something you might not have seen before. Standing back, you can also see you might not be right about something, or you take a step back and what you thought was a boulder in your path is actually a pebble. In business, too,

36

you can get so involved that when you hit a problem you don't see the answer. On the occasions when I've stepped back and looked at it, the answer has often been right in front of me.

I've had to be creative in finding different ways round things, which can be quite good fun. The way I see it, most people, who can read and write, travel through life with blinkers on, like a horse; whereas, I have no blinkers so it's a lot more work. I know it's not really like that, but it's as if they're travelling a straight line all the way, and I'm not; I'm having to go all round the houses. In one way, it seems like they're guided, which is quite nice: they don't have to put in the effort to push their brain ten times harder, like dyslexic people do. But there's a freedom to see other things that they miss.

I've always had all these abilities; I just chose not to use them before. I didn't realise I was making that choice at the time, of course, but when you start using them you can see, with hindsight, what you did. Everyone has these abilities, but we've been conditioned to travel down one path. Years and years ago, we had to use all of them to survive, and I've had to use them because of my dyslexia. The education system doesn't take any of this into account: it's designed for the masses. And yet, in the twenty first century, we're having more and more trouble teaching people to read and write.

CHILDHOOD

When I think of my childhood and growing up, I think of constant pain. I've blocked a lot of it out because it hurt so much. We were on the bread line, and my parents were hard and strict in a lot of ways, but we always knew we were wanted; we were just never told. It wasn't a bad house to grow up in, and it wasn't a bad upbringing – it was just the pain of the dyslexia. I had nightmares until my late teens. The main recurring one was being in the middle of a room with people all around me, laughing at me. The world was my enemy.

My dad worked constantly. He was holding down at least two jobs: delivering milk from four in the morning until about ten or twelve o'clock; then, in the afternoon, going and doing gardening jobs, or that type of thing, to bring money in because my mother never worked. I remember, when I was a young kid, him going without dinner so we could eat, and then he would go and do all that work. We always had the bare essentials; there was never a lack of food for us. He was the most amazing guy I could ever want to know.

My nan and my dad were strict. I could wrap my mum round my little finger but I never tried to get away with much with my dad. I got put on report from school quite regularly, usually because I hadn't done some homework (guess why that was!). I'd ask my mum not to tell my dad and she'd sign the paperwork and not tell him. In some ways, I was petrified of him. I'd get a good hiding if I was found out. That's the way it was in those days in the working class background we were from. It would be a good hiding with his hand or his milk-round book. You'd struggle sitting down afterwards. It wasn't a beating, but it was a good hiding. They weren't the easiest parents and, unfortunately, parents can screw you up, but they tried their hardest; I know my dad did. I always say we got dragged up instead of brought up and that's a bit mean, but I do feel like that. He didn't do too badly, though: he installed morals in me and the will to carry on. I suppose Mum, as well, in her own way.

My mother is quite dyslexic, as well. She had a very good upbringing, but she needs care most of the time. Dad used to look after her when he was alive. I love her to pieces, but she's a challenge, and I remember that from when I was a child. On my fifth birthday, I was playing with my sister, climbing in and out of a bedroom window. It was an old house and the windows opened outwards with a wooden bar in the middle. For quite a while, we were climbing out of one side of the bar and in the other until I slipped on the sloping roof and fell onto a concrete path. As I was falling, I heard my sister shouting, 'Come back, John!' I think I was unconscious for a little while and then I remember I started to cry because my arm hurt. My mum heard me crying and came outside. The next thing she did was pull me up by my broken right arm, while I squealed!

I felt loved, but it was never shown; some hugs when we were younger, but then no affection – nothing touchy-feely. She did try her best when I was in my first year at Charles Dickens School and having 'extra English', as it was called. Two or three times a week she would come up to the school and try and help me read, and some of the other kids as well, like a classroom assistant. She did what she could. She always showed that I was her favourite, and that, to a big degree, has always hurt my brother and sister. They would tease me because I couldn't read and write, to hurt me because they were jealous, I suppose.

My nan brought us up when we were very young. My mother was just there. My nan was my hero; she was the world to me. I'm the youngest of three (my brother is four years older than me, my sister two years older), and Nan was our 'mummy'. She was well into her eighties when she died. I was just ten and it really hit me hard. The stress of her dying brought me out in boils all over my body, then they turned to carbuncles, which were unbelievably painful. I had about five across my back, and I've still got the scars. It was then that I started to go out with my dad on Saturday mornings on the milk round and help him deliver. I used to go to my nan's every Saturday, and I think it was a way to take my mind off things. He never paid me any money for that because it all had to go into the bills for the house, but I used to get tips from the customers. I used to make £1.50 - £2.00 a week, which was a lot of money in those days. It taught me that if you don't get off your arse you don't get anywhere.

I was twenty-nine when my dad died, but that's still young to lose a parent. Ironically, my dad is still my hero. He was a grumpy old bugger, but he's still my hero. I found out when I was sixteen that he wasn't actually my father. My mum had an affair, and I'm what came out of it. My brother and sister knew for years before I did, then my sister had an argument with my mother one day, and she just turned round and said, 'If you don't shut up, I'll tell him.' Then I latched onto it and got told. My brother and sister knowing for years before I did was like someone laughing behind your back and you knowing nothing about it for years and years. With struggling with dyslexia, that was like a double blow.

My mum told my dad that I'd found out but we never did speak about it; we just never needed to. My mum even left my dad and my brother and sister, and moved in with my biological father (he just recently died; I never met him) when I was about two months old. One day, Dad went round and asked her to come back and look after the other two and said, 'I will treat John like my own son.' And he did, right up to the day he died. He never ever showed that I wasn't his, and I still feel amazing guilt about it. Not so much now, because I had counselling a few years ago and when he died, but I feel indebted to him for taking me - somebody else's bastard, as you were called in those days – and treating me no different, with the dyslexia as well, which was like compounding the whole thing. I don't think I could do it. He was one hell of a man.

For years he sat down with me and tried to get me to say the alphabet all the way through. One night, when I was about fourteen, he managed it. Nobody else had been able to do that. It took a lot of bloody hard work and I responded because he was trying. When I managed it, I was extremely emotional about it; it was an amazing experience - I still struggle saying the alphabet now – and I looked up at him and he had tears in his eyes. I can still see it now. My mum never tried to do that. I wasn't his child. It still hurts.

In the last couple of years of his life, we became amazingly close and then, within weeks, he was dead. He complained for some months before about a stiff neck, and he was a typical guy - wouldn't go to the doctor – and then, all of a sudden, he practically lost the use of his whole body. It was an abscess on his spinal chord. He got rushed up to hospital and they operated, but it left him paralysed from the neck down. He was ill for seven weeks and basically gave up. He was a proud man and did not want to go on like that. I could see it and I remember pleading with him not to give up, but he'd had enough. Since then, I've replaced the memories of him in the last few days and weeks and, instead of seeing those visions (which I can still bring back) of him being a wizened old man (he looked about ninety at the end and actually looked better when he was in his coffin), I remember him as he was before he got ill. He died on a Friday night, of septicaemia in the end.

The hospital asked if we would donate his corneas. He was only fifty-nine but, because of the septicaemia, they were the only things they could use. Giving them, to give somebody else sight, helps me. He had lovely eyes, and I love the feeling that part of him is helping someone else. I can't even remember what colour they were. I can't remember what he sounded like either, which is a shame, but a lot of stuff gets shunted to my subconscious to make room for me to operate on a daily basis. My brain has to get rid of so much information in the past to keep up with what I'm doing today, and stay crisp.

Normally, I went out on a Friday night and drank ten or twelve pints, but the night he died something was telling me not to. It was unusual, but I decided to stay in and save the money. About eleven o'clock I got a phone call and it was the nurse. I could hear Mum crying in the background, and the nurse told me he'd died. My world just fell to pieces.

My dad had been transferred to a London hospital because his condition was so unusual, and I had to drive up there in his car to be with Mum. I managed to get hold of my sister, Dawn, just as I was going into the hospital, and I can still hear the sound she made: it was blood curdling, the cry she gave out; it was almost like an animal in pain, and I'll remember it to the day I die. For a while, we were all quite close because of that – adversity bringing people together.

When my dad died, my only support was gone. I had known he was always there for me, and knowing that was normally enough. I did have bereavement counselling, but I put a lid on my feelings so that I could survive. I don't think it did me any good to put a lid on them, but lots of people do it to be able to survive.

I was in mainstream education. I started in 1970, when I had just turned five. I went to St Mildred's, a small school in Broadstairs. They didn't know about dyslexia in those days and at that age, if you struggle with something, you start doing everything you can *not* to have to do it. The memory that comes back straight away is being in the freezing cold corridor with my face in the corner because I'd been playing up. If I really got frustrated, I'd sometimes lead with my fists. The anger would come out like that, and I think that's very typical of dyslexic people. It was all because I couldn't do what they wanted me to do. I was out in the corridor constantly, getting further and further behind. It was usually only me ever out there. I was disruptive because what they were asking me to do was so difficult. Sometimes I was just *asking*, because I was struggling so much with it, and I was being quite loud or shouting because I was frustrated and telling them I couldn't do it and needed help. But with thirty-five or thirty-eight kids in the class and one teacher, it was an impossible situation. I was making noise, being disruptive, and they had to get me out of there to teach the rest of them who could learn.

Then, of course, in the playground, the kids in my class started to tease me and blame me, saying when I played up they got told off as well. It was only a few of them, but it only ever is. It was hurtful. They constantly called me names, mainly 'stupid'. I wasn't very outgoing but I had three or four really good friends. I was lucky: it would have been appalling if I'd been in that position and no friends at all.

If I'd had one to one teaching, being so much younger I might have managed the phonetic system; I don't know. More than likely it wouldn't have worked, but it would have been nice to have had that option. The brain is so much like a sponge at that age, and maybe I could have taken more in. I remember trying to read to my parents because the teacher said the more I did it the better I'd get, but it didn't happen. They thought it would all fall into place, but they got it wrong.

I remember some of the teachers saying, 'John, just go away. You're just stupid. Come back when you want to learn to read and write.' It's people's ignorance at the end of the day, and it's actually their problem: they're frustrated with themselves because they can't teach you, or whatever, and they put it onto you; it destroys people, it really does.

I thought everything was like the cartoon version of 'Beauty and the Beast':

walking through the woods there's this nice leafy lane, and then there's the other one, which is dark, with thunder and lightning everywhere. For me, it was like being in that awful bit all the time, with things coming from everywhere and you've got to try and process the information. Most people are walking through the little glade with leaves falling down around them and it's all, from my point of view, beer and honey. Now I know it was just my perspective on things, but it was so relevant to me at that time with those problems. It was all lightning and thunder everywhere, and dark, and there were gremlins all around, coming to get me and calling me 'stupid'.

Because my birthday is in September, at the beginning of the school year, I was sixteen and a half by the time I left. It would have been so much better if my birthday had been at the other end of the year. As it was, I was there longer at the worst time for me, because the last two years of my schooling were a complete and utter waste of time. I was actually working three and half days a week, evenings and weekends, doing washing up.

I started at The Charles Dickens School in 1977, and it was a bit of a rough school then. The kids who left the year before I started had burned down the staff room, it was that bad. If you were walking along in the corridor and there weren't any teachers about, the older lot would punch you or take you round the corner and bully you. I was lucky because I was already the size of a fourth year so I didn't get much physical bullying - I could fight back physically, and I did - it was more verbal, which is actually in some ways so much worse.

At that time, there was not a lot of money in schools, and a few of the teachers did try to do what they could do, but with maybe thirty seven in the class there was a hell of a lot for one teacher to deal with.

There were other kids struggling with reading and writing, but they could do better than I could. I had lots of extra English but it was all the written word and we didn't even do the sounds: a word would be shown to you and you had to try and remember it. Well, dyslexic people's memories are not good.

I was diagnosed with dyslexia at fourteen, and then they started using phonics. I definitely couldn't do phonics and, by then, I *so* wanted to get out of the system. My behaviour wasn't the best, but it was by no means the worst. I'd be sitting in the lessons just doing as little as possible and talking. (I knew I couldn't be too bad because if my dad found out there would be hell to pay.) I'd get lines for playing up! It was like, *Oh, you've got an open sore there! Let's poke it a little bit more!* Some of them, I will dislike 'til the day I die, because they caused me a lot of problems with that type of thing for a lot of years.

I remember a new teacher, who didn't know me from Adam, and I was mucking about because I was in a French class when I couldn't even read and write. If you're struggling with English, what chance have you got with French? He came up to me one time and said, 'You are nothing but scum.' I launched into him verbally – swearing - and got sent to the headmaster to be caned. I was about fifteen and I was so annoyed about it I said, 'You are *not* going to cane me! I was sticking up for myself. Yes, I was mucking about, Sir, but I really went off on one when he called me 'scum'.' My father never knew and my mother still doesn't, to this day. The headmaster said, 'Right, well, I'll talk to the teacher about this and you might get your punishment later.' Nothing ever happened.

There were no parent/teacher evenings at the schools I went to. My mum sometimes went to the school to speak to the teachers; my dad was always working. She did what she thought was right, but my dad actually did more. Other than that, the report came home and that was it. Some said I tried hard and that was the best I could do because of my problems. I don't remember what else. Most of the teachers were overstretched and they had to leave me behind and work with the others, who had a chance of learning something. It did me a lot of harm for a lot of years, and I felt bitter for a long time because of it, but they just had to push me through the system and get me out the other end. Some were nasty, some did what they could, and the others told me I was stupid.

I was towards the top end of ability in rugby, though. It was something I found easy, and it was an escape. It was just so physical, I suppose I could take my anger out by bashing someone out of the way. It was the one time I felt a winner - putting an egg shaped ball down on the ground over a try line! But I felt part of a team. I felt a part of something. It was the only time people actually wanted me on their side. I was a fast runner, bigger than most of them, so I could barge my way through.

Every few matches, the teacher rotated the captainship round three or four of us, and I was quite verbal on the pitch. Not many people put themselves forward for it but, if I was good at something, I would. The rules were so much easier then: get yourself through those fifteen players, and it doesn't matter how you do it as long as you don't punch them in the face; that was about it.

I was always there on sports day and quite often won. The only problem was that, apart from a few of us, everyone was rubbish at sports in the house I was in. So I was always in the 1500 metres, the 800 metres, shot-put, 100 metres and relay. We always won relay. The four of us just clicked: we were so smooth at the teamwork of passing the baton. I'd love to remember their names and I just can't.

I was a very fast runner, not far off the 100 metres record at the time, but nobody pushed me in that direction. Maybe my teachers were just existing themselves, but I could have possibly been a famous runner. I was also a very good darts player when I left school. I could have become professional, but I didn't think I could do it because my confidence was so low, and nobody encouraged me in that direction either. It might not have worked out, but that's beside the point.

School taught me absolutely nothing. Those are meant to be the best days of your life; they were the worst days for me. There were fun bits because I had mates there, but that was out of school. Every single moment in school was a complete and utter waste of time – every single moment. Without realizing, the system crushed me and stopped me from learning. It almost crucified me. Getting up every morning, knowing I had to go, was when I got into the habit of just existing, just to get through it. I switched off to survive. There was no other way round it. I couldn't *not* go to school. I went for fear of what would happen if I didn't: I had my dad at my back. I dropped through the net, and that was it, pure and simple. The best day of my life as a kid was the day I left school.

AN EARLY START

I didn't learn anything for quite a few years after I left school because I didn't think I could. I had a job from the time I was twelve and kept that job until I was seventeen. I was a kitchen porter – grand title for a dishwasher. Being a kitchen porter was not the highest mentally challenging job in the world, but it was something I could do really easily, and I was extremely good at it. There were other kids my age working there who could read and write with no problem at all, and they just couldn't do the job; maybe they didn't want to do it. It would normally take two people to do it on a Saturday night; I was doing it on my own. They told me I was the best kitchen porter they'd ever had, and it was just so *alien* for me to hear that. *And* I was getting paid dam good money: at thirteen I was earning £1 an hour, which was a lot for a kid in 1978. I'd do lots of hours and they'd round up the last hour, if I'd gone fifteen minutes or so into it, because I was good at what I did. So I always had money in my pocket, and from fourteen onwards I was doing about thirty hours a week. It was a waste of time me being at school; I should have left at fourteen.

When I was at school, I couldn't better myself; it was an impossible situation. When I was working, I was doing something I could do and wanted to do, the big motivation being wages at the end of the week. I was earning money, buying my own clothes: I was pretty self-sufficient. By around 1981 I was earning about £35 a week; then I left school in '82. At one time, I was earning more than my brother – it didn't last long, but for a little while - and he was a full-time chef.

Right after I left school, I went to college for about four months in Broadstairs. It was called a 'Preparation for Work' scheme, to help people like me. Some of the young adults really excelled there, but for me it was a load of cobblers. It was an extension of school – picking up a book and reading! I mucked about, got asked to leave, and went and got another job. I was told I could come back and do my exams but, by that time, I was working in a bakery, getting there for two o'clock in the morning and working until midday. I'd leave the house at one o'clock in the morning, cycle from Broadstairs to Ramsgate, which was about five miles, and then cycle back home for about one in the afternoon. I remember the government at the time saying, if you wanted work, get on your bike and go and find it, and that's what I did. I started in the bakery in 1982 and it was '88 when I changed jobs.

It was quite fortunate because at that time, in the bakery trade, you didn't have to put in an application form: you walked into the bakery and asked if there was a job there; if there was a job, they taught you in-house. I learned the recipes in there, how long a loaf needed to be in the oven and so on. It was just a job, but I enjoyed it in quite a few ways.

When I first left school, I did want to join the army and serve my country. I actually went in to sign up in a place in Margate. I was going to sign my name and the guy advised me not to do it. He said that because of my dyslexia I could never go up the ranks, so that was in some ways a dream gone.

Britain, as a nation, is the best one in the world, but we have our problems. So does every individual, and the nation is just one big individual. At the moment, as a nation, we're just a little bit too inward looking and just existing; it's no different than individuals. We were the most powerful nation in the world for hundreds of years, and we took a big knock back when we lost the Empire or, without getting into politics, gave it back where it should have been in the first place. In the past, I felt ashamed to be myself and, as a nation, it's no different to the individual: I think we feel ashamed that we had a massive empire. We have to get over that and move on. As individuals we're really brainy, but as 'the public' we're incredibly stupid and like sheep. We have to love ourselves and our country: not the government or the way the country is set up, but the land itself – the actual earth. We're a very old country; why are we making the same mistakes all the time and not learning from our history?

I've always loved my England. It's mine. The land is as much me as I am it. I've never played rugby for England, but when I put on my England top, I am England. I have a red rose tattooed on my left arm: that is the English rose. The grass always seems greener somewhere else and, nine times out of ten, when you get to where you think the grass is greener, it's not. Quite often, you come back to where you were before and love what you've got. In my case, I'm English. I can't find the words to say how proud of England I am. I don't think I could be happy anywhere else. Yes, we have problems, but so has every other country. There's no perfect country in the world; it just looks better from the outside. There are a lot worse places and not a lot better.

I always enjoy my holidays in Britain more than I do when I go abroad. The few occasions I've gone, it's been very nice – lovely weather – but after about five days it's as if my left arm has been cut off. I miss the rolling countryside; it smells different from anywhere else. England owns me. You are your country's child.

I quite often wonder: if I had been born in the time leading up to the First World War, would I have been as brave as they were then? You don't know that unless it happens to you. Would I have made the ultimate sacrifice in dying for my country? I hope I would have done, if it had come to that. I've never found that out about myself because of what happened when I tried to join the army. In some ways, I regret not joining. Looking back though, I don't think I would have become the person I am now if I had. In the Forces you have to be moulded in a certain way for it to work. I think I would have become a different person and lost the person I am now.

Working in the bakery was something I could do without too much difficulty. I didn't feel this at the time but, looking back, I really started going into myself and just existing through the day. When I went to school and had the work outside, I was a lot busier and I did have friends of my age. I wasn't, by any means, the most popular at school, but I had my own friends. Even though school hadn't been fantastic, there was someone there; you felt a little bit protected. When I left, I knew that was it: it was me, with my degree of dyslexia, against the world. I knew I had to make it on my own. I couldn't depend on my parents because they were just surviving themselves in those days. That's when the depression started. It had been simmering in the background and then the shock of suddenly realising it was me against the world was bloody scary at sixteen. I was getting up when most people were going to bed; that wasn't good either. Even though you do it day in and day out for years, the body never does really get used to those hours - it didn't for me, anyway. Years before, when you could leave school at fourteen, there were easier channels into other things, like National Service and apprenticeships, that were gone or coming to an end when I left school. Fortunately, I found an apprenticeship in an indirect way and they taught me how to bake bread. I wouldn't know how now!

You know really, really deep in your brain when you're just existing and not creating your full potential. There will be a lot of people knowing what I mean by that, whether they're dyslexic or not. Thousands upon millions of people get up in the morning and just go to work because they have to. When I was about fifteen or sixteen and a kitchen porter, there was one time the veg. chef hadn't come in for some reason and I had the offer of doing the veg. work for that night. It could have been an opportunity for me to progress and most probably be a good chef, but I thought, *no, no, I can't do that because I can't read*. Somebody could have helped me with that - one of the other chefs could have read things to me - but I didn't have the confidence, so I pushed my self-destruct button and said I just wanted to stay a kitchen porter.

I worked in three bakeries after I left school: one, I got laid off; one, I left because it was more just work experience; and the last one – the main one – I stayed for about six years. Then in 1988, I became a road marker – painting lines – because it was more money and I was just married.

EMOTIONAL FALL-OUT

I was going into pubs and drinking at fourteen. I was getting served because I looked older. I would go down to the pubs where my brother used to drink over those years, and I got to know his friends, although they were quite a bit older than me. I had fewer and fewer friends my age and as time went on, I drank more. I was lucky that it never overtook me. Fortunately, I've never taken drugs, but I can understand why some people become alcoholics. There's that nice moment when you forget, when you almost lose every faculty in your body; it's the one time you're at peace. But I suppose I had to keep on carrying on because nobody thought I would make anything of myself and, deep down, I must have been saying to myself, *if I do go down like that, they're right*. I didn't realize I was saying that to myself at the time; it was something deep-seated, and it kept me going, somehow.

When I was in my late teens, I thought I could enjoy myself, and I suppose I did in some ways, but I was going more into myself as the years were going on. I talked to people – I was chatty – but I had no confidence; it was destroyed. I could understand, at that time, when I heard of somebody committing suicide. Someone I knew from school committed suicide when I was in my early twenties. He'd split up with his girlfriend and, one night, just got in the car, put a hosepipe to the exhaust and went to sleep. I remember thinking he was a prat, but at the same time I was thinking, *that must be so peaceful*. I was tired of fighting. I suppose, subconsciously, I pulled myself out of it, but for people who are dealing with dyslexia and the brain not working in a normal way, the energy of just getting through the day is sheer and utter hard work. The only time I felt safe was in that split second before I passed out, drunk. That was the only time. You just want the pain to stop.

Unfortunately, there seems to be a higher percentage than usual of my school year who have gone - suicides and drugs. It was a rough school. In my class of thirty-five or thirty-six, I think four of the parents owned their own houses, and even that was very unusual.

It was rough all round in those days. Looking back, as a country we seemed to have lost our way and there was not much money around to help. The mid sixties were the last few days of the Empire, and then that was it: the whole country was looking for its identity again; we went down and we had to come back up. The year I started work, we had the miner's strike and the Falklands War.

The only thing I can say is that I had a guardian angel somewhere, who steered me until I was ready. My view of religion is not quite how the Church sees it, but I would say I'm a religious man in my own way. I firmly believe in life after death, and that you go to a better place. But you can make the best of this one while you're here. I do believe I had a guardian angel, who was steering me away from the roads I could have gone down, and none of those roads were nice. I didn't realise at the time, but there was *something* subconsciously stopping me and steering me to the point where I couldn't go on the way I was, and since then I've led my own life, which is a damn sight easier.

I like to think my guardian angels are my nan and my dad. Whether that just makes you feel better in yourself and it was my own subconscious moving me away, I don't know. It makes me feel better to think that it was either my nan or my dad guiding me for my own well being, because I certainly wasn't doing anything else, subconsciously, for myself. I was just pressing my self-destruct button, and I thought I was pressing really hard, but I wasn't. Things could have been worse.

There are roughly five million dyslexic people in this country. Our gaols are full of people who struggle with reading and writing, whether they're dyslexic or not. In some ways it makes no difference, because it's still just as bad. If that had been caught earlier and they'd been helped *then*, I think our prisons would be a lot emptier than they are.

By the time I was fourteen, I was going down a path that I think would have ended up in gaol. I was starting to steal from shops, smashing things, and knowing people who would steal cars. I don't think I was far away from stealing the cars with them. That would have been 1979 or 1980 and cars were incredibly easy to get into.

Fortunately, a policeman managed to catch me and talk to me just before I started really stealing from shops in a big way. I wish I could remember the policeman's name, but I can't. He caught me doing something – dangling on a branch, causing mischief, trying to break it, just getting into general trouble, and I remember him saying to me, 'Carry on the way you're going, John, and you'll end up in gaol. There are a few guys in there who will really love a young boy like you.' I knew exactly what he meant! That turned me away from the road I was going down.

The local bobby knew all the little shits, and I was bordering on being a little shit. I never got caught in anything, fortunately, although, I almost did once. Two or three mates were with me, messing about on a six foot high wall that divided the bottom end of the back gardens between the rows of houses. We were throwing stones at cats, or something, and someone must have called the police because we saw a policeman – actually just his hat - waiting for us at one end of the wall; we turned the other way and there was a policeman's hat at the other end too! We started running and I was last, behind the others. I thought, *if I get caught I'm going to be taken home and really get into trouble, and it won't be nice.* My friends carried on running and they got caught, but I jumped down into someone's garden and *exploded* through their back door. The mum was cooking – she screamed – and I went running through their lounge/dining room where the kids were sitting, watching telly. Fortunately, I don't think the husband was there because it wasn't the end of the workday. I exploded out of their front door and *ran*! I knew if I got caught I would be in big trouble and it would be painful. I've never run so fast through someone's house and down the road in my entire life – I was gone! I ran to the recreation ground and stayed there for about an hour, mucking about with some other friends (who hadn't done anything!), and then I went home as if nothing had happened.

My friends were good: they never told the police who else was with them. They got frog marched home and their parents were told; they were in a lot of trouble for a week or two – it's called 'being grounded' now - but nothing else was done about it, and I got away with it. I don't feel good about having invaded somebody's house, but there was no other way round it at the time. In those days, people didn't lock their doors so much, fortunately, or the mum would have been after me with the frying pan.

I was a little sod, and it may have been a cry for help from me, I don't know. I thought everybody had it in for me and the world was going to keep me splattered on the ground, underfoot, and every time I tried getting up it would splatter me down again. After a while of being knocked down and having to drag yourself up, you get up just a little bit slower every time. The biggest problem is you actually hate yourself.

I didn't really have a girlfriend in those years because my confidence was so low. I lost my virginity round the back of the bicycle sheds when I was about fourteen and then it was years before anything else happened. When I left school, my confidence just got less. There was some kind of safety net at school, even though some of my worst experiences were there.

I didn't go to the pub in the week because I had an early start every morning, so in some ways the early start was good. Then, just after turning eighteen, I passed my driving test, which was quite a major achievement. I had to spell out the registration number. I asked for a pen and paper to write it down because I could copy it, but I couldn't say what it was, and I got that look – prejudice. I'm dyslexic and there are people who are prejudiced against me. It happens everyday; it might be subtle but you get that look. It's humiliating, and it's the same with racism, sexism, or anything: it doesn't make you feel good. It makes no sense to me. We're actually all human; surely, we cannot be that different.

I failed the first driving test because of a misunderstanding of what he asked me to do – maybe not concentrating enough - and I passed the second. I actually had a puncture half way through, and I still wonder, to this day, whether the driving instructor just felt sorry for me. He was about to cancel the test and two blokes came out of a house and said to him, 'If we get that done quick can he carry on?' He said, 'Yes, if you can get it done in the next couple of minutes.' And they did it, and I passed! The driving instructor went round afterwards and gave them a few quid to get a drink. It made me feel that there are nice people out there. In some ways that was a new experience for me. Most of the time, I just got that look when I said I was dyslexic, and I still get that look, but now I know it's their problem that they're like that.

I don't think I ever went out together with my first girlfriend. We just got drunk together and would then go back and have sex. I slept with a few girls that I worked with or met in the pub, but I wasn't confident enough to have a relationship.

I met my first wife, Fiona, when I was twenty-one. She was eighteen and in the sixth form. She had a Saturday job in the same bakery as me, and I asked her out. She seemed highly intelligent to me; she was doing her A-levels and seemed to have the world at her feet. Although it's a highly skilled job, I was just a baker with all those weird hours. I remember seeing some *beautiful* sunrises in the summer, though.

Some of the bakeries I worked in had a 4am start and, in the middle of the summer, it's actually getting light at that time. Even though I'm not the most religious person in the world, those amazing sunrises did make me think it's not a mistake - this world being here and my place in it. Looking back, they were important moments. I could say I was touched, if that makes sense. I still get up at that time in the morning to do work, even now, and to see those beautiful sunrises.

Fiona's parents just tolerated me. They had 'the look' when they knew I was dyslexic, as well. Nothing was ever said to my face but I was shown in other ways, like the time when Fiona got her A-level results: we hadn't been going out very long; we walked back to her house one day, and her parents gave her the letter. She was nervous opening it, of course, but she'd passed everything and I was really pleased for her. I remember feeling that there was something wrong but I stayed a while, anyway, and then when they were getting dinner ready I said I'd go. Literally, as soon as I walked out of the back door, I heard the champagne corks popping and it was a weird, weird feeling. Some people might say they just wanted to celebrate alone with their daughter, but it would have been kinder if they'd waited until I was out of the gate and out of earshot. I don't know why they did that, but it was horrible walking up the steps from the back door, knowing that as soon as I was gone they started their celebrating. It was like a poke in the eye.

Fiona worked for a firm of accountants after she left school, which was never good enough as far as her parents were concerned; they were always pushing her to go to university. And *I* was definitely never good enough: they were disappointed that she married me; they thought that she'd married beneath her. That crushed my confidence even more, if that was possible. I couldn't understand why she wanted to marry me.

She was twenty-one, when we got married, and she carried on working for a while. Her parents owned a hotel in Margate, at the time, then they sold that and moved down near Canterbury, and we had a lot of contact with them, which didn't help. And of course, they never liked my parents either, for different reasons, one being that their backgrounds were too different.

There was always tension between my parents and Fiona, too. They felt that Fiona was trying to change me. They tried to like her but it was hard going. I don't understand the class system - I think it's stupid - but I suppose you could say Fiona's background was upper working, if not middle class, so it was a shock for my parents that I was marrying somebody from a different class. Fiona's parents felt she was lowering her sights, and I think my parents picked up on that. My mum admitted that she didn't really like her. It's never easy being pulled two ways and distance grew between my parents and me, because I was with someone who didn't get on with them. Fiona didn't like them, I felt I had to choose, and you have to choose your wife. I think that's one thing that contributed to me leaving in the end. That was one reason, another was her parents, and then us just growing apart, both of us not willing to try and work it out. The marriage didn't have much of a chance.

At the very beginning, Fiona would stick up for me. One time, when we were doing up the house, her mum said something to her about me. I don't know if it was to do with dyslexia or that I wasn't doing enough, because I was working in the bakery then. I did rewire the house we were moving into on my own and got it certified at the end. I'd never done anything like that before, but I always found that type of thing interesting and not too difficult. Anyway, I remember her mum walking out as soon as I walked in because Fiona had had a go at her about it and stuck up for me, and she did that a lot at the very beginning. We definitely did love each other at one stage, but we were very much chalk and cheese.

I remember Roy, my brother, Fiona and I were coming back from a wedding or something on my side of the family, and we stopped off to see Fiona's parents at their cottage outside Canterbury. Roy needed the 'loo' – a 'number two', shall I say – and didn't notice that there was a Portaloo there. The toilet was screwed down, but it wasn't plumbed in - no water in it or anything. He did what he had to do, then came down and said he couldn't get the toilet to flush. Then it all dawned on us! We had to go up and unscrew the toilet and get this enormous *turd* into the Portaloo. We were laughing and laughing, and Fiona was heaving and laughing and panicking. I don't think her parents have ever forgiven us, and that may be one reason they don't like my family!

We were married about six years and during that time my daughter, Katy, was born. Life changes forever when you become a parent. It's the best thing that can happen to you. I can't think of the words; it's only other parents who can understand what I mean by not being able to explain how I feel. It's the best thing. But I didn't think I deserved it.

I always knew that Fiona would go to university, which she did, just after Katy was born. She gave up her job and went to train as a teacher. She met a lot of mature students, started circulating with people who were well read, which, of course, I'm not, and we just grew apart. I always knew that she would move on and, in those days, I was just surviving. The marriage wasn't working and there was only my money coming in. Everything was such a struggle. When the self-esteem is so low, you do everything you can, without realising it, to keep yourself in the pit because, ironically, that's where you're most comfortable – in pain, emotionally. I'd never known anything else. In arguments, she was extremely sharp and quick (I still struggle with someone who's quick in arguments; somebody with dyslexia can't come back as quickly), so I'd always feel that I was losing the argument even if I really felt that I was right. I was very frustrated and it felt like I wasn't being heard. I used to lose my temper and, in an argument, as soon as you lose your temper, you've lost the moral high ground anyway. I suppose, subconsciously, I was hitting my self-destruct button to get me out of it, whether that was right or wrong.

Ironically, if I'd still been with Fiona, I wouldn't be the person I am now. I was a completely different person with her. I was so amazed that she wanted me. She's got her faults, but she was a well-read girl and, in some ways, she could have had her pick. I was just so amazed that she was in love with me. The family break-up was a self-fulfilling prophecy because if you tell yourself - or are told - something often enough, you believe it and start creating that prophecy. I didn't think I deserved a family; I didn't think I deserved Katy. What you think about most comes to be, and that's the road I took myself down; I was busy surviving in my own torture; that's all it was - I was torturing myself. And this happens time and time again with dyslexic people.

When Katy was three, I walked out. Fiona thought I was having an affair. I wasn't. I really started going down. I was just existing for existence sake. I saw Katy to begin with, then I wasn't allowed to see her much at all. Ninety percent of divorces are never resolved in a nice way, but I think Fiona was being manipulated by her parents. I know for a fact that they said, 'Well, he walked out on you so he walked out on Katy, as well.'

Then the Child Support Agency got involved and was taking one hell of an amount of money off me. My wages looked like a lot of money: it was 1993 or '94, and I was clearing about £240 a week. But then my rent was about £80, the CSA were taking £90, so that left £70. It cost me about £40 a week in petrol, because I had to drive from Margate to Maidstone, daily, to go to work, so I was left with about £30 a week to cover gas, electricity and food. It sent me into spiralling debt. The last place I wanted to be was in a flat where I could hardly afford to turn the heating on. I was getting really, really low, so I went out and got 'legless' and saw people and they, in their own way, kept me going. But the only way I could finance that was by getting into debt. It kept me sane because if I'd just been in the flat on my own, I think I definitely would have done myself in. It was just a 'no win' situation.

It didn't get too bad, financially, for about a year because I still had the house, which we'd had while we were married. Fiona was living with her parents and had left it to me to sort the house out, which I wasn't really up to at the time. Fiona had dealt with all that type of thing before – forms and deeds and legal papers. It's only in the last ten years that I've had the confidence for that kind of thing; I didn't think I could do it before. With hindsight, it wasn't a good thing, but you take the easy option because your confidence is so low.

I tried to stay in the house, but I couldn't afford it. We were in negative equity at that time - the housing market had plummeted - but, fortunately, I managed to get somebody to rent it, and that paid the mortgage. It was a couple of years before my dad died, and we got close again; he was quite supportive; Mum was just relieved. I went back home for a while, until I got a flat.

At one time I had a little car, which was our car when we were married and then, one day, Fiona wanted to borrow it. I said she could, but that I needed it for the next day to go to work. She took it and never gave it back. Fortunately, the company I was working for let two of us borrow the company truck for a while, until I was able to get hold of another car. Fiona had put locks on ours to make sure I couldn't take it back. She was winning all the time because she was comfortable, still studying and had her parents' support.

I could hardly survive on the money that the CSA left me with, but I did for a while. In the summer, when they assessed me and took £90 a week, I was working almost seven days a week. But then in winter, in wet weather, you can't put the road markings down – they don't stick – so then I was on a small basic wage. I would ring up and say, 'Look, I'm not earning so much money now that it's winter.' And when I'd got them to realise that, they'd say, 'Write a letter. You have to put it down in writing.' I'd tell them, 'I'm dyslexic. I can't do it.' And because I wasn't paying so much, they were saying I was getting into arrears. The arrears eventually amounted to about £5,000.

When they sent letters, I often broke out in a cold sweat. I wondered what they were asking for or going to want now. I put some of the letters in the bin; I just couldn't cope with it. I rang them up and told them again about my dyslexia and that I couldn't read them. The guy told me I had to write a letter to them to tell them that! I just said, 'Sorry?' and he said, 'Oh, I see what you mean. Can somebody help you with it?' There really wasn't anybody and he had no answer to the problem - no help, nothing to offer.

It doesn't seem to me that dyslexia is taken seriously as a disability. Lots of people think it's an excuse for not doing something – basically, laziness. That's been said to me more times than I care to mention. Some years, in a twelve-month period, I wouldn't be able to count the times on my fingers and my toes. It's so unjust, but as a dyslexic you do realise the world isn't fair and you have to put a positive slant on it, if there is one. You have to try and change how you look at it, for your own sake, but I didn't know how to do that then.

There were times, when I was at my lowest point, that I would be there with alcohol, drugs and a knife in my hand for a good hour, just wanting the pain to stop. I wasn't seeing my daughter, who meant so much to me, and being taken for so much money was like another stab in the heart. I was getting fleeced so much that my wages were not enough to pay for my flat, and every time I would ask the agency if somebody could come round and help me out with it, they just said 'no' and 'can't your family do it', which they couldn't really. There was nobody who could help and I was in this spiral down.

It's like being punished because you're a guy, and you would hear on the telly that blokes had committed suicide over the CSA. As far as I'm concerned, the CSA should be prosecuted for the way they treated the easy targets. The actual reason they got set up was to get people who weren't paying, but they went after the easy prey, which I was one of. It was criminal: they destroyed people's lives. There are some real arseholes out there who just walk away from their kids, and they get away with it.

I remember ringing them up and saying that I was getting charged all this money, Fiona was claiming benefits because she was still at university or had just finished, and I wasn't even seeing my daughter. They said that wasn't their problem and if I was upset with something I had to write a letter, then it would be official. I told them, again, that I was dyslexic and I couldn't. They did suggest I go to their office. At the time it was in Hastings, though. I was living in Margate and they were only open during the week, when I was trying to work to pay the money they were taking off me. It was a bit of a 'catch 22'. Maybe I should have gone down there, but I wasn't exactly thinking straight at the time. It was another way the State dropped me through the net, and I was left fending for myself. I didn't expect them to do it all and commiserate, but, *go on, give me something, for God's sake!* The System has always let me down, and it's still letting people down.

I was drinking ten to twelve pints a night at the time, spirits as well; working, going to the pub, coming home at two in the morning four or five times a week just to forget. I slept around quite a bit in those three years; you felt wanted for a while, but there was always that feeling of being nothing and nobody.

I was lucky if I saw Katy once every three months. Fiona had got a job in the New Forest and moved there with Katy, so I had to go there and stay in a hotel over the weekend, which was more expense added on to what the CSA was taking. Fiona refused to let me see her more often, and her parents wanted Katy to have nothing to do with me. I tried, when I could, to ring up every night before she went to bed, but I wasn't even allowed to talk to her some nights. It felt like my money was good enough, but I wasn't. I do believe Fiona was being pushed by her parents into things she maybe didn't want to do, and she was angry and hurt the same as I was, but between the ages of twenty-eight and thirty-one I had nothing and my Dad died. It wasn't the best time of my life.

During that time, I was coming home, one night, from a nightclub where you could always guarantee getting a 'one night stand' if you wanted one. You had to be twenty-five or over to get in and it was well known for divorced people. You didn't have to try that hard to have a bit of fun for a night! I was walking home, very drunk. I sat down on someone's garden wall because I was staggering - one step forward and three steps to the side - and fell asleep, literally: I fell into their rose bushes without waking up, even though I later found I'd cut myself quite badly and had quite a few scratches. I'd left the nightclub about half two in the morning. I don't know what time I sat on the wall - it could have been five minutes later or four o'clock - but it was winter. The next thing I knew, I was being woken up, hearing a voice and being poked by some old woman with her walking stick. She was hitting me and shouting, 'Get out of my garden!' It was about half five and I was *frozen*. My legs were still up on the wall so all the blood had run out of them, and I just grunted. She carried on shouting, 'Get out of my garden! People like you should be arrested!' And she was poking me with her walking stick all the time, really hard, right in the chest, on my arm, my face – anywhere she could. I was trying to get the walking stick away from me, and I was hung over, the worse for wear, freezing cold, and trying to get my bearings, because it was still dark, and I didn't know where I was, at all. I started saying, 'I'm going! I'm going!' I was trying to get my legs off the wall and out of her rose bushes while I was getting scratched and she was still poking me. If she had been in the war with that walking stick, Hitler would have given up straight away!

I tried to get up and, because my legs were completely numb, I just collapsed down in a heap again. She was still poking me, shouting, 'Get out! I'm going to call the police!' Actually, I'd have been half way to China by the time she got back in the house to call them because she must have been in her nineties, bless her! I was trying to drag myself up on the wall and get the blood back in my legs to get them working. It was excruciatingly painful, and I had to drag myself along the wall on my arms. I don't know how long I'd been asleep there, but I was so cold the muscles in my arms weren't much good either. I must have been asleep a good hour or hour and a half, and I'm surprised I didn't get hypothermia or frostbite because there was a frost that night. I just got drunk to forget, and it could have been so much worse: I could have been mugged or kicked to death; anything could have happened to me. Or the walking stick could have ended up in my eye!

Even when I got out onto the pavement, that old girl was still trying to get hold of me and whacking me up the back with her stick, even though she had real trouble walking. She beat me for well over five minutes before the blood came back and my legs started to work. I had bruises all over my arms and torso. She was really old, but she had fire and she knew how to look after herself! In some ways, I'd love to have spoken to her because somebody with that much fire in her most probably had an amazing life story; she could have been in the war, dropped behind enemy lines – who knows? I did think about going round and apologizing a few days later, but I didn't like the thought of being beaten with her stick again!

That was about thirteen years ago, and I doubt if she's still about, but I do apologise to her. In a weird way, she most probably saved my life. Who knows how long I'd have been asleep there if she hadn't come out? Maybe it was my guardian angel at work again. At the time, it would have been a relief to have died; there were so many times I did not want to wake up and face it all again, but it wasn't my time to go.

It was six o'clock when I got home, and I was still really cold then. I had to warm up slowly, and then I got into a hot bath. I don't know *how* I managed to get up out of the rose bushes. I've never been that cold before or since and the *effort* to get my body going was unbelievable.

Round about that same time, I often went in the casino at Ramsgate to sober up after the pub or the club (I was a *social* member of a Druid drinking club because the drinks were cheaper!) because you used to get free coffee in the casino. Betting on the tables is exciting and you forget your problems, so I can understand people getting addicted to it. Fortunately, I didn't. I set myself a limit of losing fifty quid and stuck to it most of the time. I used to play the roulette wheel and the last time I ever played I went in with about twenty quid and came out with about seven hundred and fifty. I'd probably lost more than that in all the times I went in before, but luck was with me that night and I beat the odds.

It all helped me survive by escaping for a while. Whether it was going out getting drunk, gambling or watching television, it was all escapism – existing without having to think about things.

Katy remembers …

Before my mum and I moved to Fordingbridge in Hampshire, when I was between five and six, my memories of my dad are very patchy. I was three when we moved to Broomfield from Margate immediately after my parents split up, and I don't remember my dad ever coming to that house, although he might have done and I was just too young to remember. I do remember him calling me and saying he was driving past. I'd stand at the window, watching him pass in his van, and he'd wave out of the window. The other thing I remember is going to his flat; I remember the layout of it perfectly.

I do have a picture of him and me (which I think is the only picture I have of that time) that I used to keep under my bed. I'm really young in the picture – twelve or thirteen months – and he's holding me; I'm looking at him and he's got this 'mental' hair that's really 'pouffy' and sticks up. We're at my grandparents' house (my mum's parents) by the log fire. At some point – I can't remember when - he found me a massive stone on the beach in the vague shape of a heart, so I used to keep those two things together. I've still got them together now. At some later stage, I thought it would be a good idea to put nail varnish on the stone, so it has random spots on it, which I quite regret now!

I remember a lot about Fordingbridge, but not much about my dad there. It was as if he wasn't anywhere because I got so used to being just with my mum all the time. I had no sense of him being near me and I'd get very upset about it when he came to see me and then had to leave. It was a good three hours drive from where he lived, and I don't remember seeing him regularly, at all. I probably did see him more than I thought I did, but it seemed an awfully long time in between visits. He couldn't take lots of time off to come and see me because he was working to keep money coming in. I never noticed anything about money, at the time, but looking back on it and speaking to people makes me realise how tight money was.

My dad always used to buy me Polly Pockets, which were tiny, plastic boxes with tiny, magnetic figurines, and there were little houses and shops with them. I loved them, and they were the only toys I played with. I had lots of toys, but I never *used to play with them. I wasn't very imaginative by myself, being an only child; I was always with my mum or my grandparents. When my mum did her degree, I was looked after by my grandma: she took me to play school and we used to do cooking or making things. I remember the Polly Pockets vividly, though. My dad probably couldn't afford to buy them for me, but every time he came he had a Polly Pocket for me.*

I had a solicitor and was still fighting to get something done when Jill, who would later become my wife, came on the scene. Just before my thirty-first birthday, she arrived on my doorstep. She was my financial advisor. She worked for Friends Provident, and I'd had a phone call from her, asking did I need to sort out my life insurance and pension. I did, so I made an appointment.

Jill saved my life. There's no getting away from it: she saved my life. She was my guardian angel, and she started writing to people and sorting out the solicitor, getting things moving forward. She actually rang up the CSA on my behalf before we were going out, and she ended up crying on the 'phone because it was just so unfair. I would not be here if I hadn't met her. I'd had three years of serious drinking, and if I'd carried on I'd have become dependent – an alcoholic – definitely. I don't know how I hung on to my job. I don't know how I never got stopped, coming out of a night club at two o'clock in the morning and leaving for work at six after about twelve pints and quite a few spirits.

Jill came five or six times and on the last occasion I asked if she'd come out with me on my birthday, which of course she did. I always say she fell for me straight away! But I think it took time for both of us. We got on well and were at ease with one another. People usually go for someone on the same level as them, and when I asked her out I did think she was better than me, but I thought I had nothing to lose by asking. I didn't realise at the time but, looking back, I suppose something was subconsciously telling me to go for it because I was better than I thought consciously. I just wanted to go out with a nice woman, and I think I fully expected Jill to say 'no'. But some people just click and it's meant to be.

We changed the solicitor and things began to change. Fiona and Katy were in the New Forest, and I agreed that we would go down there for a court appearance. In the end, even the judge was saying he couldn't see any reason why I couldn't see my daughter, no reason at all. Fiona just said 'no', so he sent us to mediation to talk about it, and it was still the same: I said all I wanted was to see my daughter, and she kept saying 'no'. She said I walked out on her and on Katy at the same time. Even *they* were saying it doesn't work like that. She always had her parents pushing her to get Katy away from me.

Through Jill's eyes ...

I first met John at 6.30pm on June 3, 1996 (I still have the diary), and we started going out the following September. I worked as a financial advisor with Friends Provident, and I had a set of clients who had Friends Provident policies. I phoned him up and said I'd like to come round and review his policies. Normally, you have to try and convince people. He jumped at it: 'Oh yes, please come round. I'm in a right mess.' It was a beautiful sunny evening. I rang the doorbell, his mother opened the door, and he came running down the stairs and said, 'Come up!' I thought, he's taking me to his bedroom already?

He was between his house and his flat, and he had a big room upstairs like a bed-sit, which was slightly unnerving, but it was fine. It wasn't exactly untidy – a typical bachelor pad – and when you looked around the room you could see he was a dad: there were loads of little things like cards and toys on the window ledges and the mantelpiece. We sat down and started talking and in no time it was as if I'd always known him.

I was filling out some forms, and he came and knelt beside me to sign them and said, 'I can't read them because I'm dyslexic.' I knew what dyslexia was, but I didn't know anything about it or understand it. I asked him if he minded if I read it out to him, and he said he was fine with that. I read it out to him, thinking what beautiful hands he had. I remember I had my briefcase open and I had a form in there that I didn't need any more; I just asked him if he minded if I chucked it in the bin. Then I realised it had my address on and I'd thrown it in the bin in a strange man's house, so I had to pretend I really wanted it after all, and took it out again. Another time, when I went there later on, I actually told him that my manager was waiting for me round the corner. He wasn't, and I don't know why I said that, except maybe I didn't trust myself! I did realise very quickly that he liked me because he used to ring up a lot for appointments!

I remember seeing piles and piles of paper under his coffee table, and I found out later that they were mostly from the CSA and bills from his house. He just had no idea what they were all about. I remember seeing another letter there from a friend of his, who had written to say that she would do his reading and writing, and he had signed it, giving her permission to do that, but I don't think she ever really did because he wasn't getting any help. I think I just offered to take all the papers and sort them out. I must have spent hours putting them all into order by date.

I phoned up the CSA and told them it was a nightmare, and they had a man on the verge of hanging himself because of it all: he didn't know where he was with it; he'd had to move out of his house; he had no money; he didn't read and write, and they were being no help. It was like talking to a machine. To be fair to them, I suppose they had so many anxious and emotional people phoning up I was just another one of them. I was really emotional – in tears - about it. The frustration was immense. I can't stand anything unjust and what they were saying didn't make sense. Their response was, 'Sorry, those are the rules.' It was dreadful, and I'm not surprised so many dads actually did take their lives. Every time they took money off him, they were taking arrears as well because they said he owed £5,700, and Fiona was working full time as a teacher in Hampshire by then.

John did the typically male thing of ignoring it. They said I had to put it all in writing - a separate letter for each change in circumstances. They would alter his payment according to each individual change. We had to trace the changes in his salary for the previous few years, and we had to prove it and get letters from previous employers. It was a nightmare, and it took about nine months to sort it all out. By the time we finished, we were in an established relationship, living together! John left his job soon after because, even though the arrears were gone, the CSA was still taking a lot of money. He wasn't earning enough to cope with it, and he couldn't afford to keep his flat. One day when he got his wage slip, Fiona had got £97, he'd got £90, and he just said he wasn't doing it any more.

We hadn't wanted to move in together so quickly – after only three months - but there was really no choice, financially. To this day, my kids, Amy and Sam, who were eight and three at the time, say they met him once and then he moved in. Sam was too young to remember, but he's picked it up from Amy and says John turned up once, with cream cakes, and that was it; he moved in!

Once Jill started backing me up, I was stronger and she could stand up to Fiona a lot better than I could because of the confidence level.

I'm still not very good if people are talking fast, and Fiona knew that and was good at it; she could tie me in knots. I can deal with it now, but I couldn't then. I'd just get angry and, of course, loose the argument.

As time has gone on and water's gone under the bridge, I still don't think either of us could forgive what's gone on, but it's not so raw now. I could stay bitter and twisted about it, but she was most probably still hurting, and she was getting pressure from her parents, which is never easy because you don't want to let them down. But let's put it this way: I haven't got any time for them, at all. We're civil to one another – just - but at the end of the day, they tried taking my daughter away from me for the wrong reasons.

Eventually, we went back to the judge, and he said that I was only asking to see Katy every three weeks for a whole weekend, and if I'd asked for every two weeks he'd have still said 'yes', so every three weeks wasn't a problem. Fiona wanted every six weeks and had to back down.

We had legal aid for that, but we had to take out a loan to clear my debts – well, Jill did. I could have walked away at any time, and she'd have been landed with it. She's an amazing woman. She believed in me, and I think she was the first person who ever did. Unbelievable! In some ways, I still can't work out why, and not being able to is like a throw-back from years ago. It's always there. I've got the tools to deal with it now. My self-worth makes me a completely different person - unfortunately, a bit fatter as well!

Things got better between Fiona and me after the court case and I was seeing Katy again. I think she understood that I wasn't trying to take Katy away from her; I just wanted to see my daughter and that's any parent's right if they haven't done anything wrong. We don't talk about anything other than Katy, but that's fine; we've both moved on.

I have to live with the feeling that I didn't really see Katy, at all, from age three to five. She comes round, now, whenever she wants and has done for years. At one stage, when they moved back to this area, she was up at the village school and used to be dropped off by her mum and picked up at night. I still feel that I missed my daughter growing up, and you can't get that back, but I've had to deal with that. I make the most of *now* and have done for quite a few years. I suppose at the end of the day, it was both our faults – mine and Fiona's – but it's not worth staying bitter; it would hurt me, and it would certainly hurt Katy.

She doesn't remember much about it. We've told her bits over the years, and I know her mother has. She remembers that on some occasions she knew that I was on the phone because she heard it ring at about the same time as I usually rang, and Fiona would say, 'You can't talk to her.'

She doesn't remember a lot of it, so I'm a bit nervous about putting this down now, but maybe it needs to be said, because it was a big part of those years. It's all a long time ago now, but Fiona did say things about me to Katy, maybe to try and get her own back because it was me who walked out.

I thought the marriage was over. I wasn't seeing anybody else. I felt we were slowly destroying one another. It didn't start out like that, but we just changed so much. I certainly did, and my perception of Fiona certainly did, and we grew apart. Maybe we didn't give each other enough time to be able to grow back together. I couldn't tell Fiona how I was feeling because I didn't know. I was just existing, and I was so confused I didn't feel strong enough to work on it, so I took the easy option.

I did talk to Fiona a short time after I left about getting back together, but by then she wasn't willing. Maybe it would have worked, but neither of us gave it enough of a chance because we were hurting so much. We can't change that. Sometimes, though, it's not right to stay with a person; sometimes, whatever you do, it just won't work. I might be wrong about it, but I think that's what would have happened and, for both our sakes, it was right for us to split up.

Katy struggled with things. Until she was about thirteen or fourteen, she felt pulled between the two us - divided loyalties. We'd get a lot of tears. Things can get blown out of proportion when it's your parents, and it was bad on occasion. She might, possibly, have played one off against the other as well. Her mum was always difficult about things, and it's a shame that we couldn't get on earlier to make it easier for Katy.

Since they moved back from the New Forest, Fiona and I have got on better. She asked me if I could hire a truck from here, and Jill and I went down and stayed the night in the house they were moving out of and helped them move back. I think that was a lovely thing, and I feel good that we all did that together, even though both of us were so screwed up in our own ways we couldn't see we were hurting Katy. After I walked out and had been gone a few weeks, or months at the most, she stopped eating meat and maybe, because everything was out of her hands, it was the only thing she could control. And she still doesn't eat meat.

I've had to learn to live with the fact that, because I left the marriage, I most probably hurt the one who really meant the most to me. I do think she'll always be mentally scarred. She's moved on, but it must hurt. It took a long time for me to come to terms with that. I don't think I have or can forgive myself for it. It is in the past and I've had to move on, but I've never forgotten the feeling that I've hurt the one that meant everything to me. I take my share of the blame for that. I hope I'm a better parent now than what I was those years ago.

I wasn't the best parent in the world before I was thirty-seven. I couldn't be because I was so confused myself, my self-respect was on the floor and my confidence was non-existent. Katy sees that I'm happy with myself now, and because I'm happy with myself I can be happy with those around me. Our relationship has got better in the last four years. Instead of pushing her away because I couldn't handle the situation and didn't think I deserved her, I'm making her part of my life. I knew she loved me, but I was so deep in myself it didn't register. Being depressed is extremely selfish because you only think about one person - yourself. When you're depressed you torture yourself and you can only feel the pain, and that's how it was for me, twenty-four hours a day. It was painful being alive, and to be able to deal with it I became a shell, not thinking about anything much.

I think Katy might have struggled with confidence herself. But since I've changed, and with the influence of the four parents (me, Jill, Fiona and Andy), I see a very confident girl now; whereas before, she was more inward. I'm sure she struggles with things. We all do, however confident we are and however much self-worth we've got, and once we get through whatever it is, we wonder why we worried about it. At the end of the day, though, Katy is seventeen now and the four people who have parented her have brought up an amazing daughter. We most probably gave her a lot of negative feedback because of the marriage break down, but we all, in different ways, gave her lots of positives too.

Whoever's right or wrong, I don't hold a grudge about anything, and I like to think that it has been a four-way thing in lots of different parts of her life. I used to hold a grudge: I felt that Fiona had everything and I didn't, the basic thing being she could read and write and I couldn't. It always came down to that – the one huge stumbling block in my life – every single time.

Through Jill's eyes

John had already initiated proceedings to get access to Katy, but he had a solicitor who was next to useless. I had a really hot one throughout my divorce, so I went to see her, and she put the case together.

On the access weekends, we drove to Hampshire on the Friday afternoon, picked Katy up from school, drove back, spent the weekend and then drove back with her on Sunday afternoon. It was quite a trip, but it meant that she kept in contact with her dad. She loved it with us because Amy and Sam were here and she was in the middle, age wise; she had her own bed in Amy's room and then, years later, she got her own room, which she's still got now. She was part of us.

She was a very happy and chatty child, but I used to worry about all the stuff under the surface. Now, she talks to me about her feelings and absolutely anything, apart from boyfriends. It was a very difficult situation because we had to keep all the fighting away from her; whereas, Fiona used to involve her a little bit. Of course, Fiona was on her own with no one to talk to, but Katy would know a lot of things that we didn't think she should know. That was just our opinion, and we weren't perfect either, but lots of things were said in front of Katy that shouldn't really have been said: angst, anger, bitterness; and that's just what we knew about. Fiona's parents were the main ones doing it. They really hated John. They tried to eradicate him from Katy's life.

I can say that Fiona was never rude to me. We're very similar in that we're both strong, professional women, and now we get on quite well really. There was a lot of hurt flying around then, but we both give as good as we get. I don't like scenes and I try to avoid them, but sometimes I just felt so angry because John's brain can't keep up with Fiona. He struggles with me, and Fiona's quicker than I am. It must have been a hard time for *her too, of course, because she was on her own with a child, her ears were being filled by her parents, and that's how people react when they're not happy.*

It got easier as time went by and the access got sorted out. There was a big difference, as well, when Andy, now Fiona's husband, came on the scene. God bless Andy! He's a lovely, unbelievably easygoing guy. The four of us had a 'pow wow', which was probably the most grown up thing we could have done. A lot of things were said, we cleared the air, and Fiona and I ended up having a hug afterwards. We really all just wanted what was best for Katy and, since then, apart from the odd little spat, everything has been fine. Fiona and Katy moved back here when Katy was eight, and Katy went to school in the village where we live. It was like a dream come true for John. I was working part time then; I looked after Katy in the mornings and picked her up from school with Amy and Sam, so John was able to see her all the time.

Katy remembers …

It was very strange when I met Jill for the first time. We went out to a place similar to 'Wildwoods' where there were massive animal structures. I was climbing and fell and hurt myself. I was crying, saying, 'I want my mum. I want to go back.' That must have been quite hard for my dad, but it wasn't because I had any negative feelings about him: it was because my mum was the only person I was used to living with.

I only remember going once to Jill's and Dad's for the weekend. I'd be about six and I was wearing my orange Pocahontas t-shirt, purple one-hundred-and-one-Dalmatians leggings and pink Doc Martins – this complete fashion nightmare! – and to top it all off, a one-hundred-and-one-Dalmatians rucksack in the shape of a dog. Amy and I joke about it all the time because she was really jealous of my one-hundred-and-one-Dalmatians rucksack.

My step-dad was in Fordingbridge with my mum and me by then. My dad and Jill came to help us move back to Kent, and I was so excited. My dad brought his van or a lorry or something, and I remember sitting in the front, Jill being there, and driving back to Kent. I was really happy.

I think it was something to do with my step-dad that we moved back because his parents were in Kent, which was nice for him, and I have some recollection of him and Jill being like the peace-makers between my parents. I'm not sure if it's right, but I'm pretty sure my mum said something about having Andy to thank for her and Dad talking properly again. I don't remember my mum and dad together with me, ever. I remember being with my mum and Andy, or my dad and Jill, but never the two of them together. Maybe when my dad picked me up they had a few words and I've forgotten because of being excited. They did have a lot of meetings without me being there, which I'm only finding out about now.

It was so much better after we moved back. Whenever I wanted to, I could call up and go over to my dad's. It was really lovely, even though it was also quite hard getting used to a stepfamily. My mum dropped me over to the house before school every morning, so, after only seeing him every few weeks I, literally, saw my dad every day, had breakfast and then walked to school with Amy and

Sam. Then I came back after school, so I was there all the time. It was a complete life change. That was definitely the best part of my childhood. I remember it clearly, and I remember enjoying myself; the rest is pretty hazy. We probably had the best merging of families that you could have: it wasn't perfect but it wasn't traumatic.

I see him less now because I'm seventeen and I have more things to do, but I don't feel any less connected. He calls me up all the time, and most of the time I miss his calls because I'm at work or school, but we do talk. We don't talk about anything in particular or useful, but it's really nice because he takes the time out of his day to call me just because he wants to. He has always been really good about calling me; he's not particularly 'lovey-dovey' and I know that's his way of showing that he misses me. I always say 'I love you' at the end of the call and the majority of times he doesn't, but then at certain times - if I haven't seen him for a really long time, or if I've split up with my boyfriend or something – he does, and it's always at just the right times. Every time I really need an 'I love you' at the end of the phone call, he manages to produce one! He's not one with words and, growing up, I don't remember a lot of cuddles, but he's very spontaneous. I might be making a cup of tea and he'll come and give me a really big hug. I initiate all the usual hugs, like when I'm leaving the house or whatever; from him, it's when you don't expect it.

I've always had a really good relationship with him. We don't even have to talk to feel that we've spent quality time together because I know he finds it hard to get out what he feels. If I want to have a bit of a rant about things, I'll do that and he just goes, 'Yeah.' It looks like he doesn't care, but I *know that he does and I know that it's gone in. I've always felt close to him – always.*

Five percent of the time, I might have appreciated something in my life, but I was basically feeling sorry for myself, and I just existed. There was no other reason – I just felt sorry for myself. I thought, *I'm so severely dyslexic, how can I operate in this world?* I didn't want to hear people say there are others worse off than me. Yes, there must be, but you don't want to hear it; in some ways it's the last thing you want to hear, because then you feel guilty about feeling the way you do.

I was angry for thirty-seven years. Why me? I would get angry about my dyslexia all the time. When I was drinking I didn't get into lots of fights or anything, though. If I'm at the stage where I'm in one, I don't walk away, but I don't go looking for them. I just carried the anger around with me. I don't think I had any self-awareness at all. I'd get up everyday and think, *yuk, here we go again.* I didn't want to get up. You get up with your stomach in turmoil, you've got a knot inside, and you just hate the thought of going to work. That all happens in the first minute of waking up – just dreading the day.

Jill is my soul mate, but I'm not the easiest person to be with, and I've pushed my self-destruct button so many times while I've been with her and done really stupid things. I just thought I didn't deserve anything: my amazing wife, my two fantastic stepchildren, my daughter. They all mean the world to me, and I just didn't think I deserved them.

On one occasion, when I was about thirty-six, I hit my self-destruct button and 'played away'. In a different life I suppose she was a nice girl, and I suppose she said things I wanted to hear. I was unfair on me, I was unfair on her, and, *my god*, was I unfair on Jill! I couldn't live with that now and things have moved on, but you do that because your self-worth is non-existent. I was destroying the good things I had. There's no getting away from it.

I met her in a café I went into one day. I drifted into something because someone took an interest. It wasn't so much an affair because nothing happened - we never got that far. I was meeting her and talking to her on the phone, so it was a matter of maybe a month or two. Jill has a sixth sense. I can't keep anything from her – she knows. She asked me if something was going on and I admitted it because I'm a really bad liar.

I find this really hard to talk about. All I can say is, I find it difficult to show and receive affection. We were brought up supposedly to be strong. It was what happened in our household. There was love there, but you just didn't show it. I find it incredibly difficult to this day, and if you're not careful you can get swept along when someone looks at you, and men are quite weak ... *very* weak!

Jill was making me feel special. She always has done and I wouldn't be here without her. There's no doubt in my mind that if she hadn't got me through I'd be dead. Still, I thought that we were drifting apart and I didn't deserve her and it was going to finish anyway, so I did what I always did and hit the self-destruct button again by being stupid enough to look, for a brief time, at someone else. I'm pleased it didn't go too far, but it's still a betrayal, and anything I say is an excuse for my particular weakness at that particular time. No excuses. I was a prat.

Jill might remember it differently, but I have to put so much brainpower into the here and now that things like that get very fuzzy, especially if they're painful. It *was* very painful: bad for everybody in the family. It took time to get my relationship with Jill back on track because it doesn't matter, at the end of the day, whether it was a full-blown affair or not; it was a betrayal and Jill was hurt. Now, we call it the 'year of indiscretion' but it was less than two months. We have a laugh about it but I don't forget how it hurt Jill. Women don't forget, but men don't either. That's being human. You might forgive, and I'm sure Jill has forgiven me – I know she has - for that stupid lapse in my life, but you can't forget because it's feelings. We were meant to be, but I tried destroying that relationship because I didn't think I was worthy of it.

Through Jill's eyes …

I remember 'the year of indiscretion' so vividly. We were working so much, we were exhausted, and we'd forgotten what it was like to have a relationship. We were trying to hold down three companies at the same time and it was work, work, work. A lot was going wrong and the stress levels were enormously high. John was not coping with things. On some days, he was so depressed I don't know how he got out of the door.

By this time, our company, 'J.A.Tipping', was actually going well because we had two blokes on board who were really good. They were older and they looked after John, as well as the company. I think the world of both of them. I was so busy and so stressed I wasn't able to worry about John, and I probably wasn't seeing everything, but it finally got to the stage where I had to drive him to jobs, and he was saying he couldn't cope any more. I phoned two major clients one day and told them he'd had a break down. I knew them really well and I could talk to them. I told them the guys would be there and would do the job, but John couldn't be contacted.

I booked a holiday to Malta and we were due to leave in about ten days. John was acting really odd. He told me about a woman surveyor who had asked him out and he'd refused. I couldn't understand why he told me that, but it was as if an awareness button had been pressed in my head: I do have a sixth sense, and something was telling me that something was going on. There was a road works plan in his work trousers, and it had a phone number on it. He has hundreds of plans of road works with phone numbers jotted on them, but I looked at that one and knew, for some reason, that it wasn't right, so I questioned him about it. At first, he said it was a site manager's number. I asked whom I'd get if I dialled the number and he said, 'I have to tell you the truth, don't I?' Then he told me he'd met this woman; she was having a bad time and he was a shoulder to cry on. This wasn't the surveyor, so I don't know if he had, subconsciously, been trying to tell me, because he completely opened up and told me everything. Things hadn't gone too far: they were very emotional together, but she realised he was in a bit of a pickle; she was no fool and she realised that he loved me, so she more or less finished it and told him he needed to be with me.

The feeling I had was the most acute pain I have ever had in my life. I never want to experience it again. It was as if someone had plunged a knife in me and just kept twisting it. It was so powerful, I could not eat. Normally, nothing stops me eating! But I couldn't eat anything for a week. The weight fell off me and I lost about ten pounds in five or six days. It was surreal - as if I was drunk: I was empty headed and light headed; that pain affected me, physically, so much.

The day he told me, we were supposed to go to a dinner later because I was taking over as chairperson for the Canterbury chapter of Business

Networking International. I phoned up a friend and told him I couldn't go because my life had just fallen apart. He was very understanding and didn't ask any questions. John and I opened a bottle of wine and I really started digging into everything, finding out what was going on. I wanted to know every single detail – absolutely everything. A lot of people would have told him to get out. It was my house and there was nothing tying me to him, but I just didn't think of that at the time; it was more a question of, how do we sort this out? It blew my trust in him completely, and you can't ever get that back. It just doesn't come back. There's always that little doubt in the back of your mind.

It was a massive shock to John. It was as if somebody, metaphorically, slapped him round the face, making him realise that his little dalliance was so much more than that: it was, actually, completely destroying me – the one person in his whole life who believed in him. He couldn't believe how he could have done it; it was as if he was two people. We had been having a heart to heart talk the previous week. He was so depressed and we were trying to sort him out. She was obviously on his mind because he said, 'I think you're going to have to let me go.' I said, 'I'll let you go when I'm convinced you don't love me any more and, right now, I'm not convinced of that at all, so you're not going anywhere.'

When we were talking about this woman, I don't know why, but I told him to phone his brother. Roy came over and he just looked at John and said, 'My god, you idiot! Why?' I think John wanted to be told what an idiot he was, plus a few other things. He wanted it. All the time he was being told he was an idiot he was feeling the victim, and it was familiar territory - his self-destruct button. He was used to being the failure and the one who was in the wrong. For him to be successful and have people think well of him was really weird for him. He loves it now, but he couldn't take it then. You couldn't praise John, and he didn't know how to praise anybody else, either.

We went out for a walk in the middle of that night; emotions were just so raw and we couldn't sleep. I lost it! I had my walking boots on, and I kicked the hell out of him. It was great! We still talk about the bootlace marks on the backs of his legs! I swiped him and kicked him, and he just let me do it. Then I told him to go away, and I just went off on my own. I needed to be alone and I hid behind a bush until he went away. It was pitch black, he couldn't find me, and he went home because he didn't know what else to do. Roy told him not to worry, to just leave me and I'd be home.

It was late spring, quite warm, I went walking and I came to a crossroads – an actual crossroads - but it was also so symbolic. I looked at it and thought, I can walk right and change my life completely (*in other words, tell John to go*) or I can go left and back to my family, with him included, and that was what I chose. I went and sat in the churchyard for another couple of hours, just calmed down and thought about things, and eventually went home to start putting it all back together again.

The hurt is still with me now, and he is terrified of leading women on. He doesn't actually lead them on, but women love John. I have a friend who said, 'Jill, you have to accept that you have a man that women love to touch.' And when I look at it like that, it's a compliment. But there have been two or three times he's got close to women again – just texts, as friends – and I come down really hard on that because he doesn't realise he's doing it.

He's a sucker for a woman who is having a hard time: they turn to him and cry on his shoulder, he'll have a cup of tea with them and make them feel good about themselves. He's learned to be very wary of that now. He's a lovely guy and the sort of man that appeals to women. I understand that because he's so big and cuddly, and just gorgeous with those beautiful eyes. When he's relaxed and smiling he's the most handsome man on this earth, and utterly loveable. But he's bloody mine!

To be fair, who, in their right mind, would put up with me?! I work with gorgeous young rugby players all the time in my business, 'Xposure'. John puts up with a lot from me.

Anyway, after that we went off to Malta and had a wonderful week. It wasn't a sticky plaster over our relationship: it was starting again, digging out the foundations, getting all the crap out and beginning to build it up again.

IN AND OUT BUSINESS

I didn't dream about having my own business; I just knew one day I would. I didn't know how it would happen with my degree of dyslexia or what it would be, but something at the back of my mind kept telling me. I remember, at school, a teacher or somebody in authority once asked what I wanted to do, and I said I wanted to own my own business one day. The remark that came back was, 'Don't be so stupid; you're dyslexic.'

Through Katy's eyes …

Before he met Jill, my dad was a completely different person because the job he was doing wasn't challenging him: he was living in the fact that he was dyslexic. When he met Jill, he came out of his shell. She convinced him that he could do whatever he wanted; she was the first person to really influence him, and she was the support behind him. One of my grandmother's friends, who was a teacher, tried to help him, so it wasn't that there was nobody before Jill who was telling him he could do it, but Jill is completely infectious and so convincing, and my dad really needed that. That was really nice for me because I saw the positive side of him come out, and that's why I've never been one of those children who want their mum and dad to get back together. Their personalities couldn't be more different and they're happier apart.

Jill does so much good for everybody, not just my dad: she's convinced me that I can do all sorts of things I didn't think I could do. My dad needed that because the rest of his family isn't particularly adventurous. Jill has taught my dad that if he wants to do something to just go for it and deal with the consequences.

Jill and I had been together about a year when we decided to start our own business in 1997. We decided, first of all, because the CSA was taking so much money and because the travelling got too much. I was travelling up to Slough everyday to work. For a while we'd been talking about me working on my own with a paint machine. I could do lots of different work, apart from road markings, with the paint machine. It's slightly specialist: you can paint walkways in factories, floors in garages, etc. We bought a paint machine, but I didn't do a lot the first year; we call it the year I had off!

Jill was earning good money and I needed a bit of time to almost try and get over what had happened and what was still happening. The court case was still going on, I was tired and my motivation was very low.

With motivation that low, why start a business? It was more of an escape. We wanted a better life, but it was the wrong time to start because I started for all the wrong reasons. The CSA were still trying to get money out of me and said I owed over £5,000. Jill fought them for me and eventually they left me alone, and actually paid me £150 back.

After that first year, I talked to a guy I used to work with and we started working together, putting up road signs. We got a few contracts that way, and that worked quite well, but one of the main problems was that if we had a slow period Jill and I made sure he had enough money and we went without. We should have split whatever was there. We were too nice in business! We supplied him with a company car as well. We grew too quickly, and because of that the cash flow went awry. That was the start of the financial difficulties we're still living with, in different ways. It was doing all right, though.

There were offices across the road, and I made the mistake of saying, 'That would make a good business centre.' Not some of my best chosen few words because Jill makes things happen, and we started Wingham Business Centre, but we didn't keep our eye on the ball. We were trying to push for the next thing without sorting out what we'd got. When we were looking at the business centre, our bank manager said it was a mistake and advised us not to do it, but to concentrate on the one main business. That's what we should have done; we'd have made it a success and been very wealthy by now. We employed about five lads at that time, and later seven.

One of the problems was that I was staying 'on the tools' because that was in my comfort zone. I thought I couldn't *run* a business because of my dyslexia so, in some ways, it was left all up to Jill, which meant she was trying to concentrate on two businesses. I used to just turn up, and sometimes I got *really* low and depressed.

We had to do a job in Herne Bay, one time, and the guy I was working with was meeting me there. I was feeling really black so I just got in the passenger seat of the car and Jill drove me over because she knew I wouldn't go otherwise. I got there, knew the job had to be done - all the boilers were ready and so on - and it was as if something clicked in my brain: we just worked together and got it all done. As soon as I got back in the passenger seat, it clicked back into the black mood. I just did what I had to do. I think a lot of people have to do that. I could feel those moods coming but, at the time, I didn't know how to switch them off.

There's a saying, you either work *on* your business or *in* your business. I worked *in* my business; I was basically an employee with my name above the door. I didn't think I deserved it. I could have done so much more.

I wasn't the best man manager I should have been either. I had such low self-esteem I couldn't control the guys who were working for us properly. They would talk back to me fast, and I'd have trouble processing what they were saying. I didn't have my finger on the controls. Sometimes I let them get away with too much because I was so internally focused, looking at the pain I was going through. I'd find it might take two guys a day to do what I could get done, by myself, in a morning.

Some of them really tried helping out by giving their point of view; sometimes it was really good and sometimes not, but at least they were trying. But without self-esteem, even if they had said there was a great big lump of gold down at my feet, I wouldn't have been able to pick it up because I wouldn't have noticed. If you're looking in, how can you look out?

Through Jill's eyes …

Everybody knows everybody in the road marking business. When we started up the road signing part of 'J.A.Tipping', a company John had worked for before was one of our first clients. There was just casual conversation going on one day, and someone said, 'Oh, Treacle can do that.' Everybody in the room went quiet; I looked up and said, 'Who's Treacle?' Nobody wanted to answer because I was pretty scary and this was in the first couple of years of our relationship when I would have done anything for John – I still would, but you calm down a bit! Eventually, somebody said it was a nickname they gave John. I didn't say anything then, but when John explained why they called him that I said, 'Bastards! That's awful!' He just said, 'I know.' Maybe they saw it as a term of affection – blokes' banter – but John had a kind of acceptance of people being nasty to him; he expected it.

We went out to do a road-marking job, one time, on the outskirts of London (I went out with him a lot when we needed two people in the vehicle). We had to park the vehicle in a very awkward position to get to the lines on the junction that we were supposed to do. This car with four blokes in it came round and screeched to a halt alongside us. John was in the driver's seat. He wound down the window and the driver of the other car said, 'Police! C.I.D! Move this fucking vehicle!' I was out of the van and I was going to go and say, 'How dare you speak to us like that!' John just said 'ok' and moved the van. People continually talked to him like that because he worked on the road. The number of times people swore - called him the 'c' word and the 'f' word - just because he was causing a diversion, was unbelievable. I couldn't have put up with it. Not only was he getting it because he was dyslexic, with names like Treacle, he was getting abuse from people because he was working on the roads.

I had dinner with some friends when I first knew John and one of them said, 'I see you've gone from one end of the social scale to the other –

a policeman and a road worker.' I was so angry I burst into tears. How can people be like that? They hadn't even met him. The other friend said, 'I don't think he'll be enough of a challenge for you, Jill. I don't think it's right.' People are blinded by their own ignorance: he's dyslexic so he must be stupid; they don't understand so they judge. It's not about being slow; it's about having a disability that makes you different.

We did eventually employ a couple of really good guys, plodders, steady workers and it could have all worked if we'd paid more attention to detail. We ended up losing both businesses. Wingham had about five employees and operated for about eighteen months. There was an old house next door, and we took that on before we'd filled the offices in the original part. Why did we? We took some bad advice. The original business centre was ticking over before that, and the road marking and sign installation company was turning over a lot of money: we had no trouble turning over £250,000 a year, so it would have been turning over a good few million by now. We could be sitting here without a care in the world, but we just didn't keep our eye on the ball, which cost us an awful lot of money.

It's the minutiae of making a success of something that trips us up. We're working on that and getting better but it's definitely an ongoing struggle. Some people enjoy that type of thing, and it's a question of finding them.

There are some outstanding employees about and they are 'intrepreneurs'. I heard that word for the first time the other day. People who work for somebody but are really excellent in their jobs are 'intrepreneurs', and I think that's a superb name. You can still be an entrepreneur but you're working for somebody and pushing yourself forward. Those people can make companies very successful, and they do deserve to be recognised and do well out of it. I had employees who took the mickey out of me, but when they worked *with* me we were an awesome team. I'm firmer now. I still don't think I'm firm enough, but that's the way I am. I try and look for the win/win for both sides, as long as I'm not having the mickey taken out of me for what I'm trying to do. You can be flexible and both win.

In 2002, we had to sell our company, 'J.A.Tipping', (the road marking and sign installation company) to try and recoup some of the losses from our other company, Wingham Business Centre, which went into receivership. It had been a dream come true to own my own business, and we lost it all. That was like losing someone very close: your companies are like your children because you give so much time to them and put so much of yourself into them. We didn't put enough time in at the beginning to get everything right; we started up too quickly and didn't take professional advice. We've done it wrong and we see the pitfalls now.

In the middle of all this, we got married. Jill had asked me to get married in a Christmas card. There was 'yes…?' and 'no….?' written in it, and I had to put a tick beside my answer. It's amazing when somebody says that they want you. I thought, *this time, I'm not going to press my self-destruct button.*

It was a beautiful hot day in June; everything was perfect. Fortunately, we have some land at the back of the house and we put a marquee there. When I had to say my responses I just started crying, and even some of the hardened ones there had a tear in their eye. I think the reason I started crying was I really realised how easily I could have let it all go because of the way I felt about myself and the journey I'd made. Life was changing in *me* and I was realising I was worth something.

During our honeymoon, there was a pause: we didn't talk about it but we knew we were going back to a load of crap that we'd allowed ourselves to get into. That's why I want to prove, mainly to myself, that I can be a businessman; that you can make a mistake in business and still be a success. That voice in the back of my head - people saying they knew I couldn't do it - is still there. I choose to ignore it, but I still don't know what will make me feel I've finally made it; I'll know when I get there.

Wingham went into receivership after the honeymoon.

Through Jill's eyes ...

When things were at their worst with Wingham Business Centre, every morning we got up and I phoned 'the bad news bank', which was an automated message of what our balance was, and I had to then plan how we were going to get through the day. There was nothing John could do about it: he wasn't a man of words and numbers; he was a man who went out and worked physically. As it was, he was loaded up with stress, trying to hold on to control of his work and the work his employees were doing, and he couldn't take on more than that; certainly not a huge mess that involved lots of meetings. Physically, mentally and emotionally, he cannot take on more than one set of things at a time, and he'd be the first to admit that. He just carried on as normal, worrying about it and worrying about me, but not taking any action. I did it all myself, and that makes you a very good business advisor because you really learn both sides of success and failure. I just did everything that needed to be done each day.

We decided to get married at the same time. I organised everything; he organised nothing! I also organised my fortieth birthday party. I do have a vast array of contacts whom I call upon, though, depending on what's needed. John's my best friend, my soul mate, I can say anything to him and he'll always love me, so it doesn't matter about the rest. When we were selling 'Tippings', I remember him phoning me and saying, 'Do you want to hear some great news?' These are the things he does, out of the blue. He told me we had a buyer for our company, and that was the best news ever.

Lots of people tell us that ours was the best wedding they've ever been to. Our church service was awesome. I was a singer in the choir at the time. I didn't sing on the day, but the choir sang all the hymns that mean something to John and me and the church was full of all the people who mean something to us. When we made our vows, John couldn't do it because he was crying and all the blokes said afterwards, 'We were all right 'til you started, John. Then we got a bit tearful.' All these tearful road workers! It was lovely – one of the best days of my life. It was so cool that everybody loved it and enjoyed themselves.

Everything was on a budget – marquee, plastic tables and chairs – and we were on a slope so people were tipping over on their chairs, which was so funny. I got drunk and sang Barbra Streisand's 'Queen Bee', a cappella. I do a good rendition of that; I really enjoy it! John did a speech, which we nearly forgot! We didn't have anything like that really planned. We didn't have anything that annoyed us about weddings: I didn't have flowers or bridesmaids, and we didn't have a photographer. I carried my bible that my mum and dad gave me; my kids walked down the aisle with me and Katy was with John – she was his 'best man' - so the whole family got married together. We had cameras on all the tables so that everyone could take pictures, and then we got them all developed so we've got some nice wedding pictures.

We went away for a week to Ireland and we were so stressed that I don't remember my honeymoon! We knew we were coming back to 'Tippings' being sold but we hadn't decided to put 'Wingham' into liquidation at that point. I was going to try and carry it on, and I think we could have made it if I hadn't been so exhausted and on the verge of a break down. Going back to work a few days after the honeymoon, I said to Amy, my daughter, 'I don't think I can carry on with this.' She said, 'Mum! For god's sake, just shut it down! You're killing yourself!' So I made the decision, just like that, to shut it down.

It actually had four directors and I went to the creditors' meetings and went through the liquidation on my own. I was the only one doing anything. You couldn't see the other three for dust! I won't talk about the other two, but one of the three was my husband! Maybe that was the way it was meant to be; maybe it wasn't the sort of thing that you could share. I also opened the sale negotiations with the company that was buying 'Tippings'. I worked through everything day by day, doing what needed to be done that day.

Even though we liquidated the business, we cleared all the debts to small businesses we'd worked with. I did all that because John couldn't have kept up with it; he's not good in a very high velocity working environment where you have to think on your feet the whole time and you're dealing with phone calls, people, things you've got to write down. I live like that all the time. He can't do that; his brain won't let him, and that's when he falls down and people think he's stupid because he's forgotten things. But he's truly amazing because

119

he'll come in with other things that you haven't thought about, very slowly but meaningfully. It's his kind of wisdom: he sees things from different points of view.

For legal reasons, I'm not allowed to name the construction company we sold 'J.A.Tipping' to. Part of the package was that Jill and I worked for them and that was fine for a while, then, all of a sudden, the manager started bullying us. I'm about six feet and weighed about fifteen stone then, and I could have knocked his block off. I did want to do that on quite a few occasions but I think that's what he wanted. We were on good money, which was part of the package, and I think he wanted to be rid of us. Every time a customer rang up about my side of the business, they always asked for Jill or me and he didn't like that. Slowly, it became more frequent. We'd be laughing and joking in the morning and ten minutes later he'd start the bullying. He didn't believe that I was dyslexic and he would say that; he said I just did it for effect so that I could get more help. Or he'd say, 'I don't know how you can work with your wife; she's just a bloody woman.' I had to keep biting my tongue. We needed the jobs because of our other business going bankrupt, but when someone says something about your wife you want to knock their head off. I had to walk away all the time, and he'd walk after me, calling me a coward.

I was struggling with that, with the failure of the other business and having to sell 'J.A.Tipping', and this went on for almost a year. Jill left. She just walked out one day and then complained to the director, who put her in another section until she found something else. I stayed a bit longer and, daily, he'd find the slightest thing. I worked from seven until five, but, often, I'd have to meet a gang some distance away, and I'd leave at three or four in the morning some days, which I didn't get overtime for, apart from weekends. By five in the afternoon, I'd done an eleven or twelve-hour day and be going home a bit early, and he'd have a go about it. I was clocking a thousand miles a week on average, running the gangs. He always made very personal comments; he just wanted to see me lose my temper. I think he was also jealous of the relationship Jill and I have, and he knew if he got me out of my job that, financially, we'd go under. He was willing to take me smacking him one for it.

It was during that time that I started having irritable bowel syndrome: at about three on a Sunday afternoon, knowing I had to go to work the next day, the pain would start. In the end I put in a complaint about him and, ironically, I was the one who got put on 'gardener's leave' (suspension with full pay while the complaint is looked into), not him.

He then started sending blokes, who I used to employ, round to my house to see if I was out working for someone else. He was always checking on me, so I became a prisoner in my own home. He would ring up, or get the guys to ring up, or I'd see his car go past the house and him looking in the window. I live in a cul-de-sac and he had to go past and then turn round. One time, I ran out and chased his car up the road. I don't know what I'd have done if I'd caught up with him. I was down and still getting kicked. Mental cruelty is the worst; I'd rather have taken a beating. As far as the company was concerned, they pulled the shutters down to protect themselves and just let him get away with it. I had nine weeks of this, including people from the other side of the business saying they'd seen me working in Canterbury, which was not true. I suspect he was bullying them as well.

There's a saying, 'If he was on fire, I wouldn't piss on him.' If I saw him on fire today, I'd walk the other way. I know it's a very sad thing to be so bitter, but he tried to destroy me. My dyslexia was part of it, I'm sure, because I struggled with the paper work in the office. He was related to someone on the board of directors, who also tried bullying me, but he wasn't that smart and I could keep up with him.

During the nine weeks it took for the complaint to be sorted out, I had to go for meetings every so often with the managing director and he said to me, one day, 'If we had known that you were dyslexic, we wouldn't have bought your company.' I asked him what that had got to do with anything, and he changed the subject. He offered me money to pay me off and get me out of the company, and I took it. I was at my lowest by this time.

When I took the pay off, part of the agreement was that I wouldn't name the company, which is fine: I don't want to say their name. They knew they were in the wrong but the easy option was to pay me off. A little while later, the manager who had bullied us had a difference of opinion with the directors and threatened to leave. They let him go, which speaks for itself, I think.

That experience almost finished me off. During the nine weeks, I sat on the sofa and sometimes had to struggle to get up. It should have been a pleasure - nine weeks with full pay – but it was the worst time of my life. I felt worthless and so helpless: I'd made a complaint and the company was protecting themselves and their image, and punishing me.

I'd get up in the morning and go straight to the sofa. Jill was working in Thanet by then, and I would want to get up and tidy the house, but I would just sit there. The kids would come in from school and I hadn't done anything all day: I hadn't showered or cleaned my teeth, or even eaten, sometimes. Other times, just before I knew Jill would be home, I'd try and tidy up and even then it wouldn't get done, so our relationship was really being tested. I just wanted to curl up and die, and I was just so tired. I slept at night but woke up more tired than when I went to bed. I'd watch television all day long because it would make the rest of my life fade into the background, but it was all crap. I felt completely worthless. To all intents and purposes, I'd been made redundant, sold one company a year before, another had gone under and left us in a lot of debt: that was the lowest point in my life. I thought my business had failed because of my dyslexia; I thought I'd been bullied because of my dyslexia. I felt like I was under Monty Python's big foot, being kept down, or, every time I got up, being squashed again underfoot. There was no relief from my dyslexia.

In those nine weeks, I thought about ending it all on a daily basis. I thought about how insurance companies don't pay out for suicides, so I thought about walking in front of a bus to make it look like an accident. But there must have been something way down deep stopping me and keeping me holding on.

After the pay off, I got a job working nights for a traffic management company in Whitstable. They knew my background and I'd got the job without a struggle. It gave me a bit of confidence that somebody wanted me. Then I happened to ring a company that used to be a client when I had my own business. They had subsequently taken their business to the company that had paid me off. I rang up to wish them a happy new year, and in the course of the conversation they told me they were very unhappy with the company and weren't using them any more because they'd mucked up a big contract. They wanted to know if I'd like to put it right. I had the chance of working for them for a few weeks, but the problem was I had no transport. The company car had had to go back and we only had one vehicle, which Jill needed for work.

They say when things are bad you find out who your friends are, and it's true. A friend of mine, who owns his own car showroom and races saloon cars as well, knew that I was going through a hard time and that I had the chance of working for some old clients for a few weeks, but I had no transport. He got a message to me, via his wife and Jill, saying to come over because there might be a car coming in on part exchange and he'd see what he could do to get me on the move again. My mother-in-law drove me over because we live in the country and I couldn't get there any other way. I went in feeling absolutely worthless. He said he'd had an 'L' reg. Vauxhall Astra come in that would cost about £200. 'Just pay me when you've got it,' he said. He knew my situation and was probably not expecting to ever see the £200. He even put a year's MOT on it. I don't know how I didn't burst into tears. Nobody had to ask him: he did it because he could and he's a nice guy, and I thank him for it. There are saints in this world and he's one of them. There aren't many people like him, which is a shame.

The job was all around the London area and the south-east. I couldn't have done it without that car and it gave me back some self-worth. It might not have seemed like a big thing to him - it was just something he could do to help me out - but as it turned out it made the biggest difference in the world to kick starting my life again. I still feel emotional about it. I was also seeing a counsellor, Peter Gleeson, then, and I used the car to get to appointments. It gave me back my freedom; it was something I owned; it boosted me up and made me feel better about talking to Peter. It was one of the biggest crucial turning points at a time when it could have gone either way.

I spoke to a few more of my old clients who had stopped using the 'company-which-must-remain-nameless'. I got so much work that I was only in the job in the traffic management company for about three weeks. I'd got my HGV license by then, which helped my confidence to go on my own again. After the pay off, I hadn't considered doing this type of work again; I just wanted out. But I suppose you go back to what you know.

A few months later, I was up and running enough to go in and give my friend the two hundred quid. He'd forgotten about it, but it meant so much to me. The car was a bit of an old 'woofer', but I took care of it, kept the oil topped up, and ended up driving it all round Kent and London. It was an Aston Martin as far as I was concerned: it saved my life. We put roof bars on it and nicknamed it 'Roofbar Astra'. I kept it until work built up and I got a little pick-up, then I gave it to my daughter.

I was back in business.

Through Jill's eyes …

Working at the company that bought 'Tippings' was great to start with, and then it all went pear-shaped and turned into a nightmare. I don't know if there was a hidden agenda: having us there for a few months, finding out everything they needed to know and then bullying us out of our jobs, but that was what they did. It takes a lot to bully me! Initially, I was busy, I was getting on all right and I quite liked the manager. All of a sudden, he started turning on me for no reason.

Six months into the job I was called into a meeting with the directors and they said the company wasn't doing as well as it should. Why were they telling me this? I was just the office manager.

'I don't know if you've ever seen this, but here's your job description,' one of them said to me, handing it to me.

'Yes, I have seen it,' I said, 'because I wrote it.' He had no idea what was going on. They'd never given me a job description so I wrote one!

Then he said, 'We're not happy with the way John's supervising on-site.'

Again, I was the office manager; why was he telling me he wasn't happy with one of his supervisors? I said, 'If you have a criticism of John, you have to have him in here and tell him, not me.' Something else was said and I replied that I understood that because I'd run my own company.

'Yes,' he said, 'and you didn't do a very good job of it, did you?'

'Don't even go there!' I told him. 'Because you have never set up a company from scratch with no capital.' That shut him up, and I just kept shutting him up, consistently. I went home livid and in tears. John came in later.

'They're reducing my salary and my rank,' he said.

I hit the roof. For one thing, I knew we couldn't manage if they reduced his salary. I wrote a letter on his behalf, saying, 'You're trying to reduce my salary and my rank. Can you tell me when these training needs arose and why they have not been addressed? Can you also tell me what you are going to pay me?' John took the letter

Behind every good man.........

Our little bit of heaven.
Relaxing in my favourite chair in Nigel and Jane's cottage in
Porthleven, Cornwall

The gang with my Mum, Katy, Paul and Amy, and Sam

Sometimes life can seem to be an uphill climb!
Dover Under 15's Rugby Tour 2007

Our wedding - 1st June 2002

and gave it to the directors. They called me into their office.

'We got your letter,' they said, demeaning John. Then they said they were going to put John's salary down by £5,000 and mine up by £5,000, to save us difficulties.

Putting my husband's salary down and mine up to compensate was so insulting. 'How dare you!' I said. 'You can't do that, and you know you can't.' They couldn't, and it was just left.

Day after day, there were comments from this manager fellow like, 'Why is it that when I come to work I'm happy and as soon as you walk in the room I feel depressed?' 'Why is it I can't talk to you like I can everybody else in this company?'

'Can I borrow your car to do a site visit?' I asked him one time.

'Borrow my car?' he said. 'You're a woman; you shouldn't even be driving. Haven't you got some typing to do?'

I was the office manager, involved with the day to day running of the company. For no reason he got somebody else in who slowly started doing all the things I was doing. He wasn't nearly as good as I was because he didn't have the experience that I had, but the sun shone out of this young man's arse!

They bullied me because they didn't want to pay me any more. At five o'clock one evening, I just got up and walked out. I spoke to the Managing Director the next day and told him I wasn't putting up with the sexual discrimination and bullying any longer. I'd already applied for another job, which I also told him, and he said he needed me in accounts until I found out if I'd got it. He was all right; he knew he had to be careful because of the

129

*discrimination and the bullying; it was constructive
dismissal really.*

GOING INTO THE PIT

I call it my pit. I wasn't in it constantly, although it felt like it, but I always knew when it was coming. It was frightening. All of sudden I could see it coming and there was nothing, at the time, that I could do about it. Something hadn't gone well or I was being made to look a prat because somebody had teased me about my dyslexia. Most of the time it was just teasing, but it's some of the worst type of humour, and it happens everyday. It would send me into my pit.

It was a feeling of despair, thinking there was nothing you could do about it and you'd always be stuck, because people say your life is mapped out and that's what you get given. I might have been dealt a crappy hand at the beginning, but even with the worst hand you can still win. But not when you're in the pit. It's just all-consuming, complete and utter darkness, and you just want to end it - go to sleep and not wake up again. I will always be dyslexic in some way - there is no cure - and when I was in that frame of mind and thinking that, I thought I had no hope of it ever being any different. It was like screaming for help and your voice isn't there so nobody can hear you. You're screaming as if your lungs are going to burst, and nobody comes to your rescue.

For a lot of years, I was caught in that pit, just existing. I remember Katy being born and I think that's got to be one of the most amazing times in your life. Everything changes. You become a parent. It should be a fantastic time, which, in some ways, it was. But I didn't feel I deserved it, so I didn't enjoy those years like I should have done. I've come to terms with that since because I can't have those years back. It's awful that I didn't make more of that because I couldn't.

I really hit my lowest point during the nine weeks 'gardeners' leave'. Jill met the counsellor, Peter, when she was working in Thanet. She was giving him business advice and she asked if he could help me out because I was really going downhill; he said he would.

He eventually took me into my pit after I had an anchor. We used the analogy of a rope tied around me and the other end round a tree. I knew the tree was sturdy and the rope wouldn't break, and it was as if I was on a slippery slope: there was the pit down there and it felt bottomless. Going into it, I could only see a few inches in front of me and it felt like there were great big monsters coming to take a chunk of me. I was thirty-six then - meant to be a big, strong, tough guy - but I was an emotional wreck. I really firmly believed that I was going to end up in a mental institution. I felt like I was in a straight jacket bouncing off the walls of a padded cell, because I had completely gone down.

I had quite a few sessions with Peter before we got to the stage of the rope. If I'd looked at the pit face on, it might not have been so scary, but it always seemed to be behind me, so I was falling backwards into it. Once the safety rope was tied onto the tree securely, there was no chance of the tree falling, and the rope was good – it was round my waist – I felt secure, I think, for the first time in my life. It was like slipping down a slippery slope - abseiling almost - but in a weird way I was safe because, even though I was teetering on the edge, no harm could come to me. That was the first time I'd felt that, ever.

When we actually looked at that pit, what seemed bottomless was only a few inches deep. My view of it was bottomless because that's what I told myself. When I dissected everything, the monsters, that I thought were huge before, were just a couple of millimetres high, because I looked at it all from a different angle.

I had to be ready in myself, subconsciously, to be able to do that. I just got to a stage where I knew I couldn't take the pain any more. You don't realise it consciously, but then you do something to change it. I made those steps, myself, to do that. Asking for help is a big thing because one way of looking at it is that you've failed, another way is that you're asking for help to make your life better. Peter was there. He did his job; that's all he had to do. He didn't have to wave a magic wand; he did his job, and he did it amazingly well. He's a good talker!

PART TWO

THE AWAKENING

PRELUDE IN 'C' MAJOR

I'm not really religious, but I do believe there is something, someone, maybe an overall plan. I firmly believe, once we leave here, there is something different for us to go on to. There was a time when I went to church most Sundays; the odd occasion - not very often - it helped. I had a chance to go on a retreat, in Aylesford, called Cursillo. I can't say too much about it because of spoiling it for other people. You go on a Thursday evening and leave late Sunday afternoon. You go through various things, not knowing what's going to happen next, and you eat and eat! There was so much food, and you get waited on hand and foot, it's worth it just for that!

The first night is very, very deep and after that you're not supposed to talk to anybody. I thought, *what have I got into?* I spoke to Jill at 7.30, Friday morning, and told her I'd had enough. She said to give it a bit longer, so I did, but all day Friday I was thinking, *what is this about?* On the Saturday we went to a service that was a laying on of hands. It was amazing: there were loads and loads of candles everywhere; it must have taken them ages to light them all. After the service, we went up to the front. The priest put his hands on my head and there was a weird sensation: my head got really, really hot - almost boiling - but it didn't hurt. I had my eyes closed, and I could feel that I was crying. It was like being touched by God or Jesus – I don't know what it was. I can't describe the experience, but it was very emotional and something I've never been able to find again.

I was about thirty-five at the time. If that had stayed with me or I'd been able to get that back, myself, it would have been a big help. Unfortunately, it didn't stay with me but I think, in the long run, it did change me. It was weird, but I wouldn't have missed it. It felt like the perfect way the world *could* be and *should* be. Sceptics might say I was just picking up other people's emotions, and I was to a degree because it was all very emotional, but some people were perfectly calm. The laying on of hands has always been associated with healing, so maybe it healed me enough to prepare me for what I was going to go through two years after that. Maybe. I don't know. It completely changed the way I viewed that weekend: a weekend that I thought was a waste of time may have helped me change my life.

Most of the problems with people in this country are that they are punishing themselves, and I was no different. Yes, I've got dyslexia, but there are a lot more people worse off than me, and a lot more people better off, in that way, than me. But my life is so amazing, and it's all down to thought.

When I was going up to London the other day, I was listening to Radio 2 at dawn and there was a Buddhist on 'Pause for Thought'. I thought they were going to talk a load of crap, because that's how I think about most religion but, actually, when you listen, you don't have to be deeply religious to take something out of it.

She was talking about the 'two arrows'. She hadn't been able to sleep properly for about seven months and was only getting one or two hours a night. That's the first 'arrow', which is almost destroying your day. But the *second* 'arrow' is the biggest thing: you start punishing yourself. (I don't know why she called them arrows; I suppose because they can hurt you.) You keep on thinking, *oh, I've only had an hour's sleep; I'm not going to be able to do anything today; I'm just so tired.* When she turned it round, took that second 'arrow' away and thought, *yes, I've only had one or two hours' sleep, but I'm not going to punish myself because of it,* she got more done than she ever thought she could on one or two hours' sleep.

I stopped punishing myself with dyslexia, and I've done more in five years than

I had in the previous thirty-seven. Ironically, in those thirty-seven years I had my own business but, my god, I ran it wrong when I was punishing myself for being dyslexic. And it's not just dyslexia, it can be anybody's self-confidence: women give up work to have babies and then they've got to go back, and they punish themselves by thinking they can't do it any more; people get made redundant, or some people are blind and don't think they can do things. When I set my mind to it, I am awesome, and anybody can be that as well. Once I'd shifted and I stopped punishing myself, it was like the world being taken off my shoulders.

I told myself for years that I deserved all the negative things I got. For some reason, when you tell yourself negative things you believe them, and when you tell yourself positive things you don't believe them. It made no difference who was in my life, I didn't think I deserved them. That was the poison in my life and I was poisoning myself. All the things people had said were most likely what put the poison in me, but I kept on re-poisoning myself. You go round in circles and you've got to break it, and when you do it transforms everything. It's finding the trigger that will do that, and it can happen in an instant. For me, the build up to what I call my 'awakening' was months, but the change itself was instant. It's all about *confidence*. That's what completely changed my life.

From the time I left school, worked and was then working for myself, there were people telling me that I *was* good enough and I *could* do these things. It's just that two particular people told me and I started listening: Peter told me one to one, and Anthony Robbins, the American author and entrepreneur, said exactly the same thing - to me and about twelve thousand others, at a workshop - and I *listened*. Everything they both said I'd heard a thousand times and said to myself a million times. They said it in a slightly different way that made me start believing it.

Anthony Robbins didn't create the systems he teaches; they've been there since the dawn of time. He just picked them up and made them his in his own way, and changed his life and the lives of a lot of other people because of it. He can only give you the tools, because there's only one person who can change your life, and that's you. I had to learn that to be able to do it for me. Both Peter and Anthony Robbins, in their own ways, gave me the tools, which I already had but didn't know I had, to get myself out of the pit. No one else could do it for me. And you think it's so difficult or hard to change, but it can be the easiest thing to do.

If you stop growing you die. You're walking around but, basically, you're a corpse, just existing, and that was no life for me. I got to a stage where I couldn't carry on the way I was, and it was either being institutionalised for a lot of years or go the other way and make the life I want. I chose the latter. Going down that other way wasn't an option for me, even though I thought it was the easier option. Actually, the easiest was what I chose. Making me the person I am now, with the confidence I've got was so easy it's unbelievable. You think, oh, *I should have done this before, Twit!*

Jill pushed me to go to the Anthony Robbins workshop the first time and then a second time. It was about £400 each and we couldn't afford it but we found the money, somehow. If you really, really want something you find a way. A classic case: lots of people can't afford a 37" wide, flat screen LCD television, but a lot of people have got them. I enjoy watching telly and I'd love one of them, but that doesn't change your life.

The first workshop felt like it set me back even more, but then again, something did click. The first day and a half definitely did set me back. In some ways, that's what it does; you just have to stick with it, because you need to confront things before you can move on, or you keep tripping over your baggage. My god,

I had a lot of that! I didn't realise at the time that I had changed: it was an ongoing thing but a major shift had happened and I stopped feeling depressed and started feeling my self-worth.

After I came back from the second workshop, which we went to some months later, there was another major shift I didn't actually realise had happened either, until I noticed I was coming home and saying what good days I was having instead of coming home and saying it had been a bad day.

The third shift happened weeks later. The workshops got me on the right road and my subconscious did the rest. It was as instant as a sudden snap of your fingers and as strong as a sudden BANG! That was my 'awakening'. I almost couldn't deal with it.

AWAKENING

The awakening wouldn't have happened if I hadn't met Jill. Life is a journey and some people you meet along the way are meant to help you. I was fortunate enough to meet Jill, and she pointed me in the right direction to meet the people I needed to meet. It wasn't conscious on anyone's part: it just happened. Lots of people say that your life is mapped out in front of you. I don't quite believe that. I believe you have choices and you can go either way, so you *can* make your life better, but you have to make the choice to do that.

The build up to the change or the awakening was months: I had gradually been feeling better and more confident. It's hard to remember what I was thinking about, leading up to it, but there was no warning. It was like walking into a wall, or somebody punching me in the face: it almost physically hurt; it was a struggle to cope with it. It was as if somebody who's been blind from birth had an operation and was suddenly able to see perfectly clearly. I thought, *fucking hell!* I remember having to pull my little pick-up van over to the side of the road, and it was a struggle to park because

I could hardly see: the tears were just pouring down my face. I bawled like a baby for a good ten minutes. I couldn't have stopped it. It was an overpowering feeling of self-worth and a realisation that everything would be all right. It was as if the world got off my shoulders and let me be me, and something was saying, *You can be whatever you want.* I grew up! I allowed myself to grow up because I had true self-worth for the first time. I believed in *me.* And I knew it would never go away. It was weird. It was almost like a physical thing, as if that part of my brain caught up and matured in me. I know it wasn't physical, but I couldn't access that part before.

Eventually, I got back under control. I think I had a t-shirt on and it was wet because of my tears. I'm just glad nobody saw me. The last thing I wanted was somebody tapping on the van window to see if I was all right.

It was an awakening - like being given a second chance. I've never met anyone who's had this happen to them, but people have near death experiences and it changes them. This particular experience changed me in all the right ways. It was like coming back from the dead because I stopped just existing. When I had that inward pressure of not feeling self-worth, I wasn't good enough in my own mind and I tried to destroy everything, myself included, because the only way I felt comfortable was being a loser without anything. Even though, in those years, I owned a house, always held down a job and had my own business, I wasn't growing. I was like the living dead. It was as if my aura wasn't there. We've all got an aura, but it's as if it took thirty-seven years for my soul to wake up because, looking back, I kept on compressing it. At the time I wouldn't have recognised it; I just knew that there was something better for my own inner self.

There were opportunities every single day of those thirty-seven years when I could have woken my soul, been the person I'm meant to be, and grown every day. You're meant to grow in your spirit every day until the day you die. In those years, I don't think I ever really appreciated a sunrise or a sunset. That type of natural beauty is literally like an awakening, anyway. Just watching something like that could have shifted me, but I didn't allow it to because I was just existing. Simple things like that can shift you, or hearing a story about somebody who's been successful and you know deep down that you could be too, but you didn't change your life. It could have been one little step to the right or the left and straight on, but you didn't do it. I could have changed when I was twelve, fifteen, ten, thirty-five - anytime. It was completely my choice not to, but I didn't know that. I had to get down to the lowest point in my life when I couldn't put up with another second the way it was. The fear and dread comes out physically until you press a switch and start to look at it, and start thinking differently, and train your brain often enough to do that. Then it will start looking for those opportunities to change, and it will bring them to you. Whatever you think, whether it's good or bad, it will come to you.

In the five years since, I still have times when I fall into just existing again. It's still very easy, if I'm not careful, to look on the black side, even now. I can see myself going down that way; I notice it straight away, whereas I didn't before, so I can stop myself, and I'm back into my awakening and enjoying the small things in life again. Sometimes it's automatic and I don't have to think about it. We all have our 'off' days when something really nasty hits us in the face and we've got to cope with it. At those times, I get the old feelings but I come out of them naturally; I don't have to force myself. I did at first, but I knew how to do it. If you do something lots of times, it becomes a habit. Other times, I have to work harder at it.

If I wanted to, I could click back into the nightmare. You make choices, and I could make that choice because nothing has changed except me. The world is the same with all the information coming at me. You can still have people trying to put you down, but you're better than them. It's a shame that you have to feel that you're better than them, because we should all be the same but, unfortunately, it's not like that at the moment. You have to raise yourself above those people. I just know I can deal with it all now.

I had that awakening and I grasped it. I know now that I will never let that go. In some ways it grabbed hold of me and I wondered what the bloody hell it was; it felt so alien, but it wasn't letting go. Even then, I was trying to get back to what I was used to feeling, but it wouldn't let me. I had to get to grips with it - start living with it. Then I really recognised what it was and that keeping hold of it was so important.

One of the best tools I was ever given was a bit of string! When you're depressed, you slump, and you're not getting enough oxygen to your brain. That is a fact: as you slump, you compress your lungs and you don't breathe deeply enough. When I was getting myself out of my depression and I had counselling, Peter told me to imagine that I'd got a piece of string tied to the top of my head and could take it in my hand and pull myself up. I thought of that and my head came up, my shoulders went back and I was breathing better, getting more oxygen to my brain. And that made one *hell* of a difference: because I was getting more oxygen to my brain, I was thinking more clearly. Something as simple as that made a *profound* difference to me. I wanted to just kick myself for not having thought of it years before. There are still occasions when I have to think of it again: loads of things are going on; the bloody phone won't stop ringing; people are calling about different jobs, and I feel myself slumping. I take deep breaths, get more oxygen into my brain, and things become clearer. Don't you want to poke people in the eye with that? Why is that not on billboards and traffic signs all over the country? 'Think of the bit of string!' It beats all the negative stuff, and it's so simple: when you're depressed, you slump; when you're confident, you feel seven feet tall. And it's amazing how much confidence comes back when you sit or stand up properly, and your brain is getting as much oxygen as it needs.

The odd time I've told people about it, you can see them grow in front of you. I carry myself very differently from before. I'm about six foot and I feel seven foot tall, but I still know that if I'm stupid enough I could flick a switch back to the way I was. And I have done it: I've felt low because of something that's happened and I've flicked that switch, but I have the tools to change it. By using that string I can switch straight away and bring myself out of it so quickly. It wasn't that easy to start with; I've trained myself.

I'm growing now, where I was wilting before. I surprise myself with what I can do now, in spite of my degree of dyslexia. I look at paperwork, although I still struggle with it. I have loads of lists in my job, and the only way to do them is with the written word. It can still be overwhelming, but I deal with it.

HIGH ON LIFE

I struggled with dealing with the awakening, at first, because everything was new: I was looking at it all from a different perspective. I had never *really* enjoyed a sunset until I was thirty-seven. How stupid is that! Nature gives you that on a daily basis, unless cloud's about and you miss it.

One Sunday, I had to work up in London - a two and half hour drive before I even got started. It was autumn, which I used to hate because I thought everything was dying, but I had a beautiful experience that day. The sun was shining on the trees and on the different colours of the leaves. It was mind blowing: the colours were unbelievable. How many other people saw that? That's given to us free; the offer's made and whether you're atheist or the most religious person, that is still free and nothing can ever take it away. There were tears pouring down my face, it was just so beautiful. It was almost like an epiphany - something as basic as that. I can't speak for anyone else but, in my opinion, if you can have that, you become a better person, because you can start looking at your everyday life and enjoy what you've got. Your life actually might be perfect but you don't see it until you look at it from that one-degree difference.

On the other hand, if your life is crap, change it for the better. One thing I learned over the last few years is, if you believe that you are stupid, or nothing's going to go your way, or you're never going to get that promotion and nobody likes you, you're most probably right because you're sending that feeling out to the world, and it feeds it back to you. Basically, you're destroying yourself. It's not other people who put you down; it's actually yourself. There was always something at the back of my mind saying, *no, John, you're better than a lot of people are telling you; you can do something with your life; you just have to believe in YOU.* But I just didn't listen to it. It was screaming at me for years and years and years and I took no notice of it. You believe what ignorant people say to you, who have got as many problems as yourself, maybe even more because they feel a failure as well, and take it out on someone else. No matter how educated or rich or well read you are, what's the point if you're not enjoying life. I haven't got it right: everyday is still a test, and I struggle everyday with dyslexia, but it's a challenge and I deal with it.

There was a company I worked for years ago. It's gone now but it was a road marking company. They nicknamed me 'Treacle', because treacle is slow and thick. That's the type of feedback I got because of my dyslexia. I've had that constantly in my life: on first impression, most people, up until recently, would brand me 'stupid' and treat me that way. 'Stupid' was the main thing I was called as a child and as an adult. In the end, the way people saw me was the way I was seeing myself, because if enough people tell you you're stupid you start believing it. I get that very rarely now, because I don't see myself that way any longer. People actually see the good things about me when I meet them, instead of the bad things.

The people who called me 'Treacle' had a problem: they were having a go at me to feel more empowered and feel better about themselves because, deep down, they didn't feel confident about themselves. That's how bullying happens: the bully's self –esteem is so low on the floor that they bully people, and the self-esteem of the person being bullied is so low too. If your self-esteem was higher they wouldn't bully you because you'd be back at them. My brain works slower than most people's, but when I did come back with something it would completely floor them, and they'd very seldom come back at me. These people are just existing.

If there was higher self-esteem there would be fewer problems in the world. Not the type of self-esteem where you think you're better than everybody, but the general feeling that you're *as* good as anybody else. People with real self-esteem are living their lives instead of just existing.

I 'woke up' when I was thirty-seven, and it can happen at any time in your life. When I had that experience, I almost got bitter about the years I'd lost, and that could have sent me down a completely different spiral. I had to watch that because I began to feel I'd wasted thirty-seven years. But I turned it around and realised that I wouldn't be who I am now without them, and probably wouldn't have had that amazing experience. In a lot of ways it was worth all those years - just bloody hard at the time.

The world is completely new for me now. I'm booming out what I want to the universe and trying to give as well so that other people, like me, don't have to struggle the way I have or in their own different ways. If you do that it comes back to you. It's the power of attraction. There will be some people who read this and think, *what a load of bollocks*, because they're not ready to move on and just click and completely change. I would have thought the same myself before I did it. I thought other people had all the advantages and I had nothing, even having to struggle with reading and writing. I'd think, *Bastards!* I was that man, but I know I will never go back to how I was. I'm a completely different person. Every single day there's something new. The world will give you anything you want if you do it in such a way that you're not trampling on people, and you're giving, so that it's a win/win situation for everybody. Like when you make a deal: you want to make money out of it and so does the other person, so you both come up with a compromise; you're both happy with it; you've both won.

On the occasion of my awakening, all the weight got taken off me. In the five years since then, other weights have come on and gone off and come on again with the different pressures of living life, but it's not the one complete pressure of existing, and knowing deeper down that you can live your life so much better but you're *stuck*. Once you get rid of that inward pressure crushing your spirit, you can handle the everyday outward pressure because it's not, actually, that much. Some days are worse than others, but most days are pretty dam good. It wouldn't be a real world if you had no pressure and no worries, at all. It happens

In the last five years, there have been trials, tribulations, lack of money and stress, but I enjoy getting up in the morning. It might be hard, physical work that I do, like the job I was doing recently: the actual site was three miles long and I had to walk most of it – going up one side, putting up signs, walking back, and then doing the same the other side. Every day, I walked ten or twelve miles. It was knackering work, but for two days out of the four the weather was utterly beautiful, and this was November.

When I got there one day, there was fog all the way round the site, but as soon as I went into the gates it was clear and the sun was shining in. It was *stunning!* And when you're in your pit, which unfortunately a lot of people are, you're so insular and enclosed in yourself you miss things like that. I had one hell of a busy day that day, but as I was walking with my wheelbarrow with all the signs in and everything, there was a beautiful blue sky, it was quite warm, and it was just amazing not to be depressed. When the alarm went off at four o'clock that morning, I groaned but I got out there and I even enjoyed the drive up there, *even* sitting in traffic going through the Blackwall Tunnel. It was frustrating but I felt so alive.

The best days of your life are, actually, only one day – the one you're living. The best *time* is this moment because you're here, living it. You're either making the most of what you've got, or not. For a woman who gives up work and brings up her kids, that can be one of the most amazing experiences. I know they're little buggers, but make the best of it. You sometimes see people in supermarkets, stacking shelves, and they're really enjoying that because that's what they want to do; maybe some of them are dyslexic, I don't know; maybe they thought that they couldn't even stack shelves so that is in no way an unimportant job. One day, that stacker of shelves could become the next Richard Branson. It's all about confidence.

I was thirty-seven when I sent my first email, which for a dyslexic is a very emotional experience. I have reading software: I click on the icon and it comes up at the top of the screen, then I can highlight what I want to read and it speaks it to me; it's like a little recorder. I have other software that has a headset. I talk into it and it writes what I say. I never learned how to write a letter and it took a long time to work out how to word an email. I will never forget the feeling of self-worth because I had sent my own email. I fill up just thinking about it. It was like going back to the first time I wrote the alphabet when I was fourteen. I got so much joy out of it.

You have to get on with things, but I quite often get the most amazing amount of enjoyment out of the smallest things: very early one morning, I was doing a small job and it was really cold; for a few seconds, I stopped and just stood there and took a few deep breaths; the feeling of the cold air going in and the warmer air being exhaled made me feel so alive, even though I had a bad cold and chest infection at the time and felt crap, physically. It's a stunning world out there; you've just got to open your eyes. For most of humanity it's like they've got their eyes shut and have got eyes painted on their eyelids so everybody thinks they're awake, but no.

Before I knew what confidence was I just survived. I recognise it in people because I lived it for thirty-seven years and it upsets me - people just surviving. We're lucky in this country because we have so many things. But we still just exist. In my opinion, there are probably only about ten percent of people in this country, maybe twenty percent at the very most, who really live their lives. The rest just survive and that is such a shame. We only have this moment.

I love talking to people. I was putting in some posts recently, it was pouring with rain and I was talking to a woman about her ducks. I can't remember how we got into conversation, but she was just so happy. She was standing in the pouring rain, talking about ducks and really enjoying it; she was loving her life. She had her problems, mind you, but she had everything she wanted. There could and should be more people like that.

There were other people around just hating the rain and hating that they had to go back to work; you could see it in their faces. They were existing; they'd switched off. They may have had a really nice family at home, which I hope they appreciated but more than likely didn't. I didn't realise what I had either, and I always thought the glass was half empty. Very few people think it's half full. That's a powerful analogy for the way you look at life. If you look at half a glass of water and see the glass as half empty, that's your life – half empty. When you see it as half full, your life is not only half full, it's full, which is weird. Every so often, I try that analogy on people and more people say it's half empty.

You think it's the most difficult thing in the world to change your thinking that the glass is half empty to thinking that it's half full. It's actually just a thought, but it's believing it that's the difficult part. I don't know if there's a God, that's for everyone to decide for themselves, but he or she made us a bit too complicated! It's amazing the number of people I meet who don't like their jobs, whinge, and don't do anything about it because it's safe. If you hate something that much, change it; do something else. We put obstacles in our own way, time and time again, and I know because I had to knock every bloody one down! I wasn't using my intelligence to get round them, which I should have done.

I'm a risk taker, amazingly enough. A lot of the risks I've taken haven't paid off, so some people might say I've failed, but I don't think there's any such thing as a failure; it's what you learn from it and I haven't made those same mistakes again. I don't have the benefit of an education and a university degree. I'm learning by living, and I really think there should be an award for being in the university of life because there are a hell of a lot of people who are failing at that. There are relatively few people passing.

My dad was always working for his retirement and he died six years before it, so he never got to enjoy it. That was a big turning point in my life, even though it was eight years before I started changing.

I never really lived my life when my dad was alive and I can't change that, which is very sad: to only exist in my own mind and somebody like him so close to me. I couldn't let him get very close because I was just existing. How could I have a brilliant relationship with him, my mum, my brother, my sister, my daughter or my first wife? I wouldn't let it happen because I didn't think I deserved it. I wasn't conscious of that at the time, although I used to always say I had a self-destruct button so maybe, deep down, I did know, but I never knew when I was pressing that button. I can never, ever press it again without realising it. It's just not possible because I've disconnected it, destroyed it, cut all the wires, busted the button with a great big sledge hammer in my own mind, and it's gone. I would have to do it consciously now, so I'd know what I'd be doing. And that is powerful.

I've thought back over my life and seen very clearly the times I've pushed it. At school there were a lot of bad times when the teachers never gave me a chance, but I pressed it because I thought, *well, I can't learn, I'm dyslexic*, so, on quite a few occasions, I just mucked about. Ironically though, from the time I was twelve, I always went out and got a job. Subconsciously, I was always trying to push myself because there was that something at the very back my mind. I think most people who have got that know it in a weird way: something keeps trying to push you forward.

Round about the time of the awakening, I heard one affirmation that made a big difference to me: **All I need is within me now.** I've had so much doubt of my own ability in my life because of my dyslexia, and the first time I heard that affirmation, I was driving along the road listening to a CD coaching course that I thought was a complete load of cobblers. Hearing that though, the tears came rolling down my face and I cried out thirty-seven years of pain. I knew that all I needed had always been there and would always be there. I was chanting it and actually hitting myself on the chest to drum it into me. I must have said it at least a thousand times that day. In the end, I stopped at the side of the road because I wasn't concentrating on driving. I was *really* hitting my chest - physically hurting myself - to get that into me and get the pain out. In some ways I suppose I also wanted to hurt myself for wasting those thirty-seven years, paralysed with my dyslexia. I was angry with myself and I had to physically hurt myself like that because of the pain I was feeling. People self-harm because of their pain: it's a relief. I'm not saying self-harm is a good thing, *at all*, and I was lucky that I just hit myself on the chest for a while as my way of releasing pain, but I understand self-harm.

There were lots of other things on the CD I could have repeated, but that was the one that was waiting. Everything you do need is within you.

I still say it and it does completely change my attitude when I'm having down days, which I still have, on occasion, because you can't feel fantastic all the time. My god, it would be unbearable – for yourself, let alone anyone else!

I was fortunate, when I was saying those type of things to myself, that I didn't have anyone putting me down. You do need a team of people around you. It could be just your husband, wife, partner, your kids, your friends, and they can help you out a lot. Sometimes they're the worst people: they can be putting you down without even realising because they might be scared that you're going to better yourself and leave them behind. But I was very fortunate that the people who were around me at the time weren't putting me down.

Up until the time I went to see Peter, there were people constantly putting me down, or that was my perception. There aren't many people in my life who have put me down, but I thought it was everybody. I once heard that there are only four bad people in the world but they just get around a lot! It's quite nice thinking that because you can deal with just four! I remember hearing that, years ago, and it actually helped in some ways. I heard the odd thing like that sometimes and held onto it.

But the biggest thing for me was saying to myself that all I need is within me now. I'd be driving along, saying that to myself, and the tears would be pouring down my face because I still didn't quite believe it. Some days, I would have to say that almost all day because even though working on your own can be nice, it's very isolated and it can make you go within yourself again.

How can seven words make any difference? But they did. I kept trying because I had no other way of going, apart from up: the idea of going down was so frightening I just wouldn't allow it to happen. I had been going the wrong way, subconsciously, but even if you're at your lowest you know you can be a better person, if you've got it in you. Even if you've got that knife close to your wrists – which I have had at times – 99.9% of people will know that they are actually better than they think they are at that moment, and they can become a better person by helping themselves. I really believe that. In the awful times you're so within yourself, so 'woe is me', you can't think how, but for me there was something always niggling in the background; I just wasn't hearing it. Although I must have heard it, somehow, because I always knew I was better. And I know I can become an even better person than I am now.

There was just the will to survive trapped in me somewhere, not being heard by the main person who needed to hear it – me. We've all got those voices shouting, *Come on! Come on! You can be better than this!* You can't see how you can be better, but it's there somewhere. I'm living proof of it. It's a lovely feeling waking up every morning not having that worry of going in that pit during the day and staying in it for days or weeks or months. It would catch me when I least expected it: something would happen or be said – just a small thing most of the time - and I wouldn't see it coming until it was staring me in the face and it would send me into the pit.

In some ways, I'm so comfortable with the way I am now that the thought of moving on is putting me right out of my comfort zone. I never thought I'd be this confident. There are still things that make me very nervous, but it's amazing the enjoyment I get out of just sitting there sometimes with the satisfaction of knowing how far I've come, and thinking, *yeah!* I know there's so much more I can do, though, and I do want to give back.

I may sound like just another 'loony' who wants to give back, but it does mean a lot to me to, maybe, give somebody the tools that I already had but got shown how to use. The selfishness in this world has somehow got to stop. I don't know how to stop it, and I don't mean that the rich have to give all their money away. I remember hearing years ago that if all the wealth got divided equally, within a very short time there would be really wealthy people again and really poor people. If somebody had given me £10,000, in the difficult times, I would have wasted it because I wouldn't have thought I deserved it.

Sometimes it can be the easy option to throw money at something, which isn't wrong, but there are other ways of giving.

I'm rich. I feel like a millionaire in so many ways, just not financially, although I will be that too, one day. When we had the business centre there was a guy, Nigel, who has a lovely little cottage in Porthleven, a fishing village in Cornwall, and he offered it to us for a week; we just had to pay the cleaners at the end. Seven years and many visits later, through the really bad times of businesses going wrong and stress levels going sky high, it's been our get away. We're so lucky to have a friend like that and both Jill and I are extremely grateful to him for the gift of being able to go to Porthleven. People in Cornwall seem to have a different philosophy of life and know how to live a little better than the rest of us. In the stressful times, being able to get to Porthleven has saved us from being ill. To us, it's almost magical. It's lovely in the winter as well; it's so windswept, and standing on the cliffs watching the sea is being one with nature. England and me are one being-ness, and Porthleven seems to bring that out in me.

I'd love to shake everybody awake. A few weeks ago I was working in Tonbridge for about a week and a half and I would say out of every hundred people who went past me, at the very most five percent were awake and smiling. I talk to anybody. Sometimes I get strange looks, but I just might make a joke and get a laugh back or have a chat. It might only be thirty seconds or a minute, but those are the people who are awake and enjoying themselves. The rest are miserable. What's the point of that? You might as well be dead. I see lots of people, in my job, going past me every day, sometimes as many as one or two thousand. I enjoy people watching just to see how they are, and most of them are not enjoying that moment.

I make the most of what I'm doing and where I am, and having a laugh with people. I was working in a car park and during one day, two people were twenty pence short of change for the metre. I gave the two people the twenty pences. They were amazed and asking me if I was sure. I said, 'If I can't give twenty pence to somebody to help them out, it's quite a sad world really.' One woman gave me nine pence in exchange for the twenty pence, but I think I made her day. At the end of the week, the change in my pocket usually goes in a charity box, but I actually think that eleven pence was worth so much more, for me. It made me feel good. Whatever I give, I get back tenfold. It's all about how you think and the way you want to be.

Even if you're wearing a high visibility yellow bib, the majority of people just blank you because they don't even see that you're there, which can be a problem if they have a big car! I can be jumping out of the way of cars and some people just make a beeline for you: it's my fault for being in the way! I can be working inside cones and people drive through the cones. There was one day when we were putting up a huge sign and we had the area cordoned off with tape. Someone walked into the tape, broke it without noticing, and then broke it at the other side on the way out of the area. They didn't notice they'd done it until I called to them. They can be so deep inside themselves, just existing, that they don't see. I know this kind of thing can't be cured in minutes, but I managed to come out the other end and enjoy even the dullest things in my life. I don't want to be in the middle of a car park putting up posts and signs, but it's what I do; it earns me money, so I make the best of it.

There are so many small things I do now that I wouldn't have done years ago before my confidence was high. Every year, we have a dinner dance in the village hall and we usually do a little sketch. It's a little performance and I wouldn't have had the confidence to get up in front of two hundred people before. Most of the time it means dressing up in women's clothing and making an utter prat of myself, but people enjoy it because it's quite funny. One year, I ended up doing the 'full monty' with five others. Imagine doing that in a little English village hall! To be able to do that – something as little as that - when I wouldn't have before, makes me realise how far I have come. I would never want to become an actor because I'm not that good, but it's fun and it takes quite a bit of bottle to get up in front of people and say your lines (which I mess up most of the time), or get your kit off. I have to say, though, I *hate* dancing to 'YMCA'! As a dyslexic, I find it difficult enough to remember the letters, let alone make the shapes!

Every so often I get a contract delivering magazines round the schools in Kent and they're just in boxes. I've got a big enough van to be able to do that and it makes a nice change from what I normally do. When I was doing it just before last Christmas, the local radio station was asking people to request Christmas songs. There would have been *no* chance of me doing that years ago, but I rang up. It rang and it rang and it rang. Now, if I'd even got that far a few years ago, within a few rings I would have put it down, but I thought, no, *I'll keep on trying until it cuts me off.* And then the program presenter answered and asked me what I wanted. There's a Christmas record I love, 'Keeping the Dream Alive', by Freiheit. It's a beautiful Christmas record that's not played nearly enough. As soon as I said that, he said, 'That is a *brilliant* Christmas song.' And he said he'd play it in about half an hour. I didn't know it was going to be the full conversation on air. I was just driving along and it came on the radio and I was listening to myself! I hate the sound of my voice on tape, anyway! But then the feeling I got totally made my day. I loved hearing the record and afterwards him saying, 'That's got me so Christmassy! It's a beautiful Christmas record. Thank you, John.' It was a small thing, but I loved it. It was a beautiful sunny winter's day, and I was just enjoying it all. I was *living*! I wasn't just going through the motions. Small things like that are really, really good. I couldn't even pick up the phone to talk to somebody before, whether it was me ringing out or them ringing in. I just couldn't do it because my confidence was so low. To be able to ring up a radio station and get through was brilliant.

Then there's public speaking, which is one of the scariest things for most people. Through Jill talking to her contacts about my dyslexia and what I do, I have been asked to do a few talks at secondary schools. I do get nervous, but I think that's good because you can feed off that energy if you're sensible and keep your feelings under control.

Most people's attention span for listening is about half an hour, and I make sure I hold their attention; I have quite a soft voice, but it can be powerful when it needs to be. I've never actually had the problem of people not listening, but I cannot *stand* it if I'm speaking and somebody in the group is talking. It goes back to being in school when no one was listening to me, I suppose. I did one talk where there were about seventy teachers in the room; they were dealing with dyslexic children on a daily basis. It was good to be able to do that because when you're a kid it's very hard to describe what dyslexia is, plus they got more of a feel for what you *can* do even though you have it. In a weird way, it was like the tables had been turned, and teachers were listening to me, for once. It was quite therapeutic!

I was also part of a business enterprise workshop in one school where there are a high percentage of dyslexic kids. They came to my table and talked to me about what I do. I was actually the only self-employed person there, and I was trying to get across what you *can* do, despite dyslexia.

The other talks were to kids a year or two from leaving school. Those were just about business because schools like to encourage a percentage of the kids to think about starting their own businesses. I'm giving another one at a college, soon, to about sixty girls, aged around twenty. It's a hard life but somebody has to do it!

One of my ambitions is to be invited to an Anthony Robbins workshop to get up on stage and talk to twelve thousand people, although I might need a tranquilliser to do it! I'd just like twenty minutes or half an hour to tell my story. I *will* meet him one day and shake his enormous hand. He is a big man - close to seven feet - and he makes my hands look like a baby's!

Until I wanted to change, in myself, and started looking in that mirror and actually liking the person looking back at me, I was stuck. I hated the person I saw in the mirror. Once I'd changed that point of view of myself, I could change the rest of my life. It had to start with myself. A soon as I started changing that feeling of I'm no good, I'm stupid, I'm thick, I hate myself, I started getting a positive attitude. It's one of the hardest things to do, with a slow, slow build-up, but the awakening happened in an instant. I definitely had relapses, but then the positive side came back and I started believing in myself again. When I looked in the mirror and, for the first time, actually liked what I saw, it was a big moment - maybe one of the biggest moments in my life. The click into being positive happened a few months before that, but then you suddenly realize it. I know it sounds strange, but because I'm so positive in my thinking about myself now and I boom that out to the universe, the universe booms that back to me more and more, and I actually get more green lights now instead of red ones!

There are still times when I allow myself to get low and start doubting myself. Then I have to work on it again to get myself back into the right frame of mind. Just recently I got quite low. I allowed my dyslexia to get to me again. One of my dreams is to be a businessman, to prove that even though dyslexia is a hindrance and a pain, you can still get round it in so many ways. But I was just feeling like a sole trader. Now there's *nothing* wrong with that; it's served me really well, but I want to keep on growing. The time of year was getting to me, as well: Christmas was over, the weather was crap, my work had slowed right down and I was having to go out and look for more in whatever one of my businesses that might be. There's loads of potential, but over those few days I'd allowed things to get the better of me, thinking, *I can't become a businessman because I'm dyslexic.* Even with the positive slant I have on everything now, all those fears rear their ugly heads from time to time, and I had to *really* work hard that time to get them out of the way. I'm not any different than most people in having fears; it's just that my biggest bugbear is dyslexia. I'd been very busy for the previous few months, and I hadn't had to worry about the next thing coming up. Then I had got to use my business side again to carry on growing my streams of income and it was … frightening.

This time, I pushed myself to pick up the phone, speak to my main clients, find out about work coming up. I also arranged with someone to work with me in my company, 'UVShield' (we cover windows with a film to shield out the ultra violet rays of the sun); and I had some meetings with the NHS about using UV shield in certain places. (There's a particular film you can put on light covers so that drug users can't inject into their veins because the film stops them from being able to find them: they can't see them.)

Some of you reading this – and I'd probably have thought the same – will think, *Bastard! He's got it all worked out and he's just moving onwards and upwards.* It may be good for you to know that, yes, I'm extremely confident about things these days, I work with my dyslexia and don't often let it get the better of me, but it still does sometimes, and then I have to work to get my hopes up again. It's an ongoing thing because everyone has bad days. There is no way that I would ever, *ever*, spiral down again, though. It cannot happen. I've explored my pit and it's not possible. The pit I thought was bottomless was just a few inches. I know that now. It was *me* who allowed myself to have bad days and there are going to be other bad days and big challenges I'm going to have to get over, but that pit does not exist. It was destroyed because I explored it. The demons from my past have been laid to rest. There will be times to come when I think I'm a complete and utter waste of space, and I'll kick myself for it, but there's no way I'll ever go down that pit that had me trapped. I created it myself, and there's only ever one pit that we create for ourselves. I'll have to keep moving out of my comfort zone for the rest of my life. To get to my deathbed, look back at my life and go, *wow!*, I have to keep growing; I have to keep going out of my comfort zone. Depression can be a comfort zone, and people stay in it because it's what they know. I have to take bad days and turn them back into good days.

I also still have to deal with people who don't understand dyslexia. My step-son, Sam, belongs to a rugby team in Dover. Just at the time they were coming into the under fourteens, the head coach went to work abroad and I was the only one who could take over. The team was potentially really good but their discipline was really poor: they'd talk instead of listening to me and you can't do that in a team sport. A few years ago, I wouldn't have had the confidence to take that on, so it was a big thing for me. I stopped playing when I was in my early twenties. I never took it seriously enough, which I do regret, but I stopped because of a back injury: every time I played, the sciatic nerve was getting trapped. When I got back into it, I realised the rules had changed: it's basically the same game but more rules, so I got on all right. Jill is the manager and she helped out a lot. We brought more discipline to the team, and then the club asked if we wanted to go on a coaching course and get the qualification. I wasn't that keen but Jill said she'd come along, as well, and do the course.

It was a Kent based course and because of the equal opportunities policy I rang up beforehand and told them I was dyslexic. When I got there – and there were a lot of people there - it hadn't been thought out how to work with somebody with dyslexia. I spoke to someone about it again, and he just said there would be no problem, they'd read the questions to me when it came to that. I said that wasn't the only thing someone with dyslexia has problems with. There was so much in the course and it went at such a speed, with video clips and things on screen, and most dyslexic people can't take in that much information so fast.

One of the main problems was that we were all put into small groups and given something we had to describe and explain: mine was lateral passing. Most dyslexics don't become teachers because they're not very good at it. They wanted this taught as a lesson, but most training sessions don't happen like that, so I think they were just ticking boxes.

We did it all over two Sundays and we had to do a lot of work writing out this training lesson. I did it to the best of my ability and Jill helped me. It didn't tick the right boxes but they didn't say too much about it, at the time.

I also had gall stones (which were very painful) and was due for an operation in a couple of weeks, but I still did all the running required.

It came to the written test and they read the questions and I got one hundred percent correct, so that showed I had the knowledge.

Afterwards, we had to go and find out how we did in the practical bit, and because I didn't do it in the way they wanted, I failed. You were classed as competent if you passed, but they didn't say what you were if you didn't pass. In my book, it meant I was incompetent, and I couldn't believe it: I was being victimised by the system *again*. Dyslexic people do things a different way. If we have to tick boxes by doing something a certain set way it's very, very unlikely it will be done that way. They didn't do anything out of malice, but it certainly made me feel like shit.

They said I would have to go back two weeks later, but I was due for the operation to have my gall bladder out then. Even if I hadn't been, I would *not* have put myself through that again. That would have been more pressure and worry, and I wouldn't have done it any better, most probably worse.

We didn't complain, as such, because we're not those kind of people, but it was unjust and I wanted to make that clear so that somebody else with dyslexia wouldn't have to go through that. They said they failed me because I didn't do the practical part the way they'd taught us, basically saying I didn't tick the right boxes. Dyslexic people don't tick the right boxes. As far as that course was concerned there was one way of coaching and that was it, which is rubbish. In coaching you have to come up with new ideas, and dyslexic people can do that because we think differently. To pass that course you had to do it their way. Jill, who had never played rugby in her life, or thrown a ball, passed that course. I played rugby for many years and I had been coaching twice a week for eighteen months before I went on that course. Yes, there are better coaches than me, definitely, and most probably some who are a dam sight worse.

A word from Sam ...

Our old coach was always lighter on his son than the rest of us, and John wasn't like that, at all: he was always harder on me than everybody else and pushed me further, which was good. He should definitely have got the coaching certificate; he's a good coach. We played as individuals before, then John came along, took over, and we started playing as a team. John was a lot more 'hands on', which the coach before couldn't be because he'd had a hip injury. John had to be careful of his back, but he joined in whenever he could, which was a lot better.

Because we 'complained'- as they saw it - a guy rang up and said he didn't see that what we were saying had anything to do with dyslexia. He thought dyslexia was not being able to read and write. Very few people realise that that's just one thing about dyslexia. Dyslexia is about how your brain works, how you have to compensate: it's a completely different way of thinking. A high percentage of entrepreneurs are dyslexic because we think so differently.

If I could make a wish I'd like a day of how a normal person thinks. I wonder: would it completely screw me up when I came back to the way I am? It's an intriguing question. I can't work out how people think and are so quick, when it takes me all round the houses to get to the same place. Not being able to read and write is like the by-product of dyslexia for me.

I take total responsibility for my life. I still fall into just existing from time to time, but that's only about five percent of the time now.

Because I consciously enjoy life so much it's become the norm. There are still so many difficulties and some of what I do is tedious, but I'm enjoying being *me*. If we could do that as a nation, even ten percent more than we are now, we'd see the happy results in every aspect of life.

Through Katy's eyes …

Over the past 5 years, since he and Jill got married, I have seen a massive difference in my dad: he's really come out of himself. In their house, we've always sat around and talked about really emotional things. It's normally Jill and me holding the conversation, just dribbling it all out to each other! Before, my dad would be present but would not really view an opinion about any situation. He does still sit there and just take things in, but now he will view his opinions and make his little jokes, or pipe up with some kind of comment that really means something – a bit you take away and think about.

I would never have thought he could go to schools and present to people, either, and do it really well: the comments he always gets are amazing and I think that's because he's a real, genuine person; he doesn't pretend to be anything more than he is, and I think that's endearing in a way.

DYSLEXIC ENTREPRENEUR
MAKING DREAMS COME TRUE

Somebody once called me 'the dyslexic entrepreneur' and I quite like that; it's a nice title. I just have a burning desire to show - even if you're not dyslexic, but you're just existing – how much more you can move on. That's my biggest desire of all. Yes, I'm dyslexic, but I want to be an entrepreneur; I want to be successful in my business.

Jill and I work really well together and we earn a lot of money but because of the financial mistakes we made, we're still not financially secure. We're working on that at the moment. Jill takes care of the finances. I've taken more interest in the last few years but even though it's figures, there's still a lot of the written word. I'm still not a millionaire – I'm ninety nine percent certain I will be one day – but riches come in many different ways; they don't just have to be money and are normally at your fingertips. Most of the time, you just have to get off your arse and stretch that little bit more and you get what you want, and you can still be nice at the same time.

I do have a chip on my shoulder about family businesses. I had to struggle really hard to get where I am, and I know I can get a lot further with a lot more struggling. This sounds nasty and I don't mean it that way because I actually laugh about it, but somebody whose parents or grandparents started up a business gets it handed to them on a plate, if they go into that business. They might have done what they wanted in the world and then gone into it. That just seems *so bloody unfair!*

This sounds so 'woe is me'! And I actually know it's not really like that: businesses are hard whether you're given them or not; a family business also comes with extra pressure because you have to carry it on, knowing that your father or grandfather kept it going and you have to make a success of it as well. But still, it just seems really unfair when someone has money behind them and is just given that. I don't mean it nastily; it's the way I used to look at it, and the chip on my shoulder rears its head, occasionally!

It's important to enjoy what you do. People stay in jobs they hate because they're comfortable with it; it pays the mortgage. There are loads of other jobs out there they could do if they really set their mind to it. Go and do it! Sometimes that means taking a wage cut and it might be a risk, but life is nothing without risks; you have to calculate them and that's the hardest part. I've taken risks: starting businesses without knowing anything about business for one! I take those risks and one of them will pay off and make me wealthy. I know that sounds big headed, but you have to feel like that for it to happen and there's nothing wrong with that.

I love the concept of 'entrepreneur'. I suppose that's what was always pushing me from deep down. I'm excited by the very word, and I really feel that's what I am but in a completely different way to most go-getters. I have to be different because of my brain working in a completely different way. However much I would try to do it the normal way, I can't because my brain won't let me; I have to go round the houses.

The word 'entrepreneur' means freedom to me. I know I can go as far as I want to in business, in my life, in anything I want to do, and the worst thing is you have to keep on coming completely out of your safety net to do it. Sometimes you're so far out it's like walking the plank; you're so far out on that plank, yet you're thinking you just *have* to do it. And then, after a while, you're back in your safety zone because you've pushed out the parameters so far that you have a bigger safety zone. Then you have to do it all over again. It is bloody scary! It's scary for people who can read and write. It can be petrifying if you can't.

Winston Churchill was dyslexic. What a great man! I would love to have sat in a room with him and had a conversation. Maybe one day I can – but not yet! Whatever you want to say faith is, one of the biggest things is having faith in yourself. One thing I've definitely learned in the last five years is to have faith in myself that I *can* do it.

A lot of dyslexic people have got such low self-esteem that they're paralysed with fear. One hell of a lot of people, I would imagine, – and this is only my opinion – are on social benefits because they're dyslexic. The school system let them down and the overall system is still letting them down. They could become amazing people in business or work career if it was changed to help them more. They might have become a brilliant entrepreneur or they could be doing what I'm doing. I'm nothing special, but I've carved out two nice little companies for myself. I'm lucky in that way: I find business very exciting and fun.

If you have enough people say you're never going to make anything of yourself, it's in some ways good to begin with saying to yourself, *I am going to show those bastards that they were wrong and I am going to stick two fingers up at them.* But you get to the stage when that is tiring because you're bitter. You can still do the same thing in a nicer way, and you don't have to stick your fingers up at them because they'll look at you and realise that they were so wrong and what they said was utter cobblers. You know in yourself that you've proved them wrong, and it's just tiring to keep thinking, *I'll show them!*

Because of all the things I had thrown at me over the years, I will give to people what I expect or would like back. When I make mistakes at work – and I do make mistakes on the odd occasion, but they're quite rare now – and you get someone on the phone who's irate, if you put up your hands, say you're sorry and say you'll put it right, how can they have another go at you? That normally knocks the wind right out of their sails. It might cost you some money, but they can't have a go at you again, unless they're really nasty people. And I do put it right, or try to. Sometimes, I don't even succeed at that, but I do try everything I can to put things right, and that's good enough. It might cost me money, but I more than likely won't lose that client because they'll come back to me again.

Since I found my self-esteem and I've been positive, my life has turned around. I'm making more money now than I ever thought I could. I'm making more in a week than people make in a month because it's what I wanted, and I've made it mine. I don't want to struggle for money and none of us needs to. We can have it all *and* save the world *and* make people happy. We *can*; we just choose not to. One person can make a difference. We lose millions of days work, as a nation, because of sickness that's really the way we feel in ourselves: we hate our jobs and hate ourselves.

I've chosen to surround myself with positive thinking people. That keeps me positive. You do need help. If you have peers you have to strive to be like, you become a better person. If you really don't want to lose contact with someone you care about, you can pull them up into being more positive. It's bloody hard work, but they may change because they see that their best mate has become so positive. I have had people say they wish they had what I've got, or that some of it would rub off on them. I like to think I make people's day better. I surround myself with successful people, in their own way, and I aspire to be like them, in my own way.

I recently joined Business Networking International, and taking that first step was massive. It's quite formal and very structured, which is scary. It's still definitely out of my comfort zone, but the only way I've grown over the past few years is by going outside it to get to where I want to be. I was lucky because Jill used to belong to the Canterbury chapter and I'd been along to that, years ago, so I knew the outlay of it. When I went to this one - and I'd been to a few other ones to see which one suited me – I knew how it worked.

It's a weekly meeting and it starts around 6.30am and finishes at about 8.30, so there are a good couple of hours of structure. I do get nervous, but it's good. At the last one I gave out six referrals, which is potential business for other people. Another time I'll get referrals. Everyone has sixty seconds to describe their business, and then a different person every week gives a ten-minute talk so that everyone learns more about what they do.

When I did the ten-minute talk, I asked people there to read it out. I wanted to show them the problem I have, which is the main stumbling block every day. I deal with it better now, and I'm not ashamed of telling people but, my god, it is amazingly hard not to be scared to tell people you've got dyslexia, or any other learning disability, because people judge you. I don't usually get bad reactions now, because of the way *I* perceive it. I come across as more confident about it, and it's just me, which helps a lot. But when you've got low self-esteem, other people subconsciously pick it up - which you don't realise but it's an automatic thing - and you get judged, mainly badly, until you turn that confidence issue on its head. Your confidence makes a big difference in the way people react to you.

I think a lot of the problems with society today are caused because personal confidence is so low. People who are outgoing and seem confident are often wearing that as a mask; most people are insecure. Without confidence, how can you perform decently in anything? If you think you have nothing to give then you're not giving, and the world needs everybody to give back a lot more.

In one business I have, I just work doing sign installation now. On the odd occasion I get asked to do a road-marking job and I subcontract it to a guy I went to school with. It's very easy to cope with and I know I could cope with more. We've been looking at premises because we do know we'll have to have employees again at some point. I could probably keep it as it is for the rest of my working life, making good money, and manageable, but it's like life: if you don't grow you wither.

If I do make the business bigger, I have to keep my eye on the ball and, for me, that means really close concentration. I'd be the first to admit I'm not the best businessman in the world but, in some ways, in this country and the western world, success is judged by how much money you've got. I earn a lot of money so if that means success then I'm a success in business. I just find it incredibly easy to spend as much as I earn and more! And I've had a failed business, but I don't think you're a success in business until you have had one go down because you learn so much from that. The hardest bit is coming back from it: it can almost destroy the self-confidence that's already dented, anyway. I started to think maybe they were right, maybe I'm not meant to have my own business. That made me feel a failure. But at the back of my mind there was always that something saying, *no, you're not.*

I run my business as a sole trader because that's easier for me: it's limited and I can deal with the odd employee or subcontractor I bring in, but there's not too much happening at once. It might be a bit of a cop out, but it's me staying in my safety zone. I do push out the boundaries, regularly, which is absolutely petrifying. But most people are petrified or worried about something most of their lives. There's always something that will take you out of your safety zone, and that is a good and a bad thing because you grow, but you're nervous about it.

I know that, with my dyslexia, I don't run my businesses how I could. My main problem, as I've said, is the detail: I don't bring it together very well. If I was to complete that part I would be more successful in money terms. I've got an overall vision of my businesses, but the minutia bores me; I haven't got the passion for that. At the moment, I use my hands so it's very physical and I can do that very well, but I know I'll have to battle with the minutiae to improve how I do business. I don't have the drive for that, whereas I have had the drive to show people that I'm not stupid. Maybe I should accept that that's all I have, but then you have to be in the financial position to hire people to do the rest for you.

I'm physically fit: I can go out and do the work with no problem at all. But do I really want to be doing that in my late fifties? No! I *could* still be doing it and there would be nothing wrong with that, but it takes it out of you, working out in all weathers for a lot of years.

I've always wanted to be able to create a family business because I want to be able to make my kids' lives easier - all parents want that – and then they've got the chance of coming into a family business and improving it, and then possibly their kids.

It's ironic that I want that even though I have a chip on my shoulder when I see other people have it! I know some really good people who have taken over family businesses, and they've worked really hard to keep it going and make it better because, in business, you find something that works well for quite a while – months or years – and then, nothing has changed but that system doesn't work any more. You have to change it slightly, or tweak it, or completely scrap it and find a new one. That will work for a while and then have to be changed again. Business is like a life: you can go along with a formula that works really well and you've done nothing to change it, but it changes, and you have to go off at another tangent. A business is a living thing and it kicks you up the backside quite often. Take your eye off the ball and something will happen!

My real interest lies in my company, 'UVShield', because that could be all over the country. I'd love to franchise it, but it's difficult to put less time into the sign installation company because it's so busy, I'm very good at it and comfortable with it. To be able to do what I want to do with 'UVShield' is going to take me right out of my comfort zone, but I want to do it to grow, myself, as a person. I want to be known as a businessman. I've been working as a sole trader for years. There are lots of people making a lot of money as sole traders, plus I have this big disability that can hold me back, but I *have* got the ambition to push myself further in business, and I do beat myself up very often about not achieving what I could. I feel I'm not giving as much as I could.

Maybe I'm on the verge of changing that because I'm definitely at a transit point. I've been so comfortable for the past five years and haven't really wanted to move on because it's been *so fucking brilliant!* But I know there's another stage that will be taking me outside my comfort zone. It's exciting. I've felt it for the past six or eight months and I'm getting annoyed with myself, now, because I'm still keeping the brakes on and not pushing ahead. I love my life. I've got rid of most of my demons. However much I conquer the dyslexia demon, though, it will always be there. It raises its head again and I have to slay it again, take my foot off the brake, go for it and grow.

Our finances are not what they should be, but I now know I can make the money I want to make. All I need is within me to do that. Our spirit in our self is all we need. Any other spirituality can be taken in as well if you want it; the important spirit for me is *my* spirit, and anything else is there for me to choose.

I thought for a long time that the world owed me a living because I'm so severely dyslexic and it wasn't fair. Well, the world isn't fair and it won't give you a living. You can go out and get that living, have the family you want, be extremely wealthy, financially, if that's what you want, and spiritually. It takes one decision, one thought to start it off. Being dyslexic doesn't stop you making that decision or having that thought. Everything starts with one thought from the smallest thing you do, like picking up a pen, to creating that multi-million pound business. It begins with a thought, and there's no difference between the most basic thought and the biggest thought that could transform you or the world. There will probably be a thought that comes up one day that will eradicate poverty or deal with global warming. I try to tell myself that, everyday, and I do forget it sometimes.

Some people say thinking about business is boring. Not me! It used to be very easy for me to make my mind go blank. I find it harder these days because I've got so many things going on with different business ventures, I'm normally thinking about one or two of them, unless I'm watching telly! That is such a magpie – it steals your time. There's nothing wrong with watching a programme or watching a video with your partner or kids, but I've wasted five or six hours at a time in the past - still do, on occasion. That's five or six hours when I could have done something to make some money without physically working. There are loads of opportunities out there, and I'm starting to get to grips with them now.

One of the ways I push my boundaries is by looking for streams of income. I want to make money while I sleep so that I'm not out there physically working. Just a pound would be nice, but to wake up in the morning and see a couple of thousand pounds has gone into my account overnight, because I've sold something over the internet, would be great: I've been asleep for eight hours and just earned two grand! There are people earning millions or a few hundred or even a few pounds while they sleep; most of us earn nothing while we sleep, but it's there for the taking.

Success in business is not in a specific area for me. Business is a game of winning and losing. I love the concept of e-bay: it's brilliant - absolutely superb; whoever thought of it has made themselves extremely wealthy. I love looking on the businesses for sale section, and I wish I were as smooth in the way some people talk so that you believe what they're saying. Most people won't make any money buying that business, but the odd one percent will become bloody millionaires doing it! They do the same things as me or the next person, but somewhere you've missed something that they did: the 'wow' factor. That's what fascinates me in business.

Money is very important because we can't do anything without it, but I don't think it's the main drive for most people who are successful: the money just comes along as a result; it's a sideline of the 'wow' factor. It looks easy from the outside but it isn't: very few people are born with a silver spoon in their mouths and it's the hunger of wanting to better themselves that drives them. People who say money doesn't matter are the ones who have lots of it, but you've got to enjoy your life to be able to appreciate it: money is not going to be enough; you've got to feel right in yourself.

They say in business that you have to have a goal to be able to succeed. I agree with that for most people, but I've never actually found a goal. I want to be financially stable but that's not really a goal; it's too fluffy and should be a more specific. It's important to think around goals, though. Some of the most successful business people give up when they've achieved their goal. They have nothing else to strive for. They were committed to that goal and when they reached it they could see nothing else.

One of my heroes, Winston Churchill, said - from childhood - that there would be a point in his life when he was needed and, my god, he was, but at the end of his life he thought that he'd failed. The Empire meant everything to him and he thought Britain had lost its standing in the world and the Americans had taken it over. He couldn't handle that; he felt a personal failure because of that. He was dyslexic, wrote books (dictated them), saved the world from tyranny and was an amazing man, but in his mind he was a failure at the end of his life. To this day, forty-two years after he died, we still have statues of him; we still have places named after him; he was voted the best Britain ever in a survey, but he felt he had failed: it's all about how you see things.

You can have everything you want and achieve everything you think you can do and still move on to something else. You might get to a stage when you'll be comfortable for the rest of your life, and then you can start giving back; that's one thing I would love to do. Even when you've achieved many things in life, you have to keep on growing by moving on to something else; even if it's growing the biggest leek in the world! Whatever it might be, if you enjoy it, go for it!

One of my ambitions is to be a qualified pilot and I don't know how I'll do it because it takes a fair bit of reading and writing, log books and so on. I don't want to own a light aircraft, but I want to have a licence so that I can hire one whenever I want to fly. When I was in my twenties, my mum bought me a one hour flying lesson as a birthday present. Once we were up, I took over the controls and I flew it around above Thanet. It was a beautiful summer day, no cross winds. In some ways, it seemed like how life should be: concentrating on one thing that you're enjoying without all the other cares. And I could do it! I loved every second of it. It was pure escapism; it felt like complete and utter freedom, and I'd *love* to fly solo. The sky is *so big*. You could go in any direction you wanted. There are rules in the sky, of course, but you just have that *feeling* of no limits. Looking back, it was very symbolic.

DOCUMENTING A DOCUMENTARY

A couple of years ago, when Jill was working for a government funded program in Thanet, the company she was working for was asked by Channel 4 if there was any business woman - which Jill definitely is - who would be willing to go on 'Wife Swap'. They talked to us about it and we got through quite a few 'hoops', shall I say, and I think they would have had us, but I was just out of the company I sold my business to, working nights for the traffic management company and trying to re-launch my own company during the day, so we backed out.

When Jill told them we weren't carrying on, she said that if they ever did anything about dyslexia, she's married to one of the most dyslexic people she's ever known. We heard nothing for a couple of years; then, out of the blue, we got a phone call from them, saying I was on their data base as being dyslexic, they were making a documentary about adults with dyslexia and there was a teacher, with a formula, who was helping people to read and write.

We had to go through a lot of interviews in front of the camera to see how we would act on camera. It looks like it just happens, but most of it is staged and you have to repeat yourself so often about how you're feeling, with questions like, 'How does that make you feel? What do you think about that, John?' Anyway, we were accepted.

The formula worked for the majority of the nine of us who were there, but for at least two of us it didn't work, at all. Jim, who is about twenty-seven years old, is a lovely guy; salt of the earth, works really hard, loves his mum, but has never really had the confidence to move any relationship forward. His dyslexia is as severe as mine. If he lived more locally, I'd offer him a job. He is so hard working and, as far as I'm concerned, he has made a success of his life. I know he would say different, but because of the way he is with his degree of dyslexia - which in some ways has affected him far more than mine and in other ways it hasn't, so it's all relative – what he is doing is success, as far as I'm concerned. School, for him, was a complete and utter waste of time.

Some of the nine there had been told they were dyslexic, but the teacher, Phil Beadle, said at the end that they just hadn't been taught properly. One girl admitted she just never went to school. She ended up learning to read in the six months of filming. The course goes on for a year, but filming ended at six months.

From the point of view of learning to read and write, the course was a complete waste of time for me. It was phonics based. I didn't know that beforehand: I discovered it once I was there, and it was disappointing. Phil firmly believed that it would eventually get me to read and write and still believes it now. I've tried it lots of times over the years. Learning with phonics works for the majority of people, but for people like me – or *me* – it doesn't work.

Phil actually asked me if it was because I didn't want to learn to read and write. I didn't strangle him! I've had people say that the whole of my life. They really believe that that is the case. I *know* that it's not, but I did have to ask myself that question because, sometimes, you're so stuck up your own backside you don't ask yourself until someone puts it to you. On the way home that night, - it was about a two-hour drive - I wondered if he was actually right: am I stopping myself from reading and writing? The answer was, *no*. It was going to take so much effort to just get the tiniest bit ahead that I'd have to give up work. If my businesses could have survived it, I would love to have been able to take six months off and done nothing else but concentrate on that course. Life won't let you do that. But even doing that, it still wouldn't work because phonics doesn't work for me. I

201

could be learning until I'm ninety, with one to one tuition and without working for a living for the next forty-eight years, and I'd be a *minute* bit better than I am now.

If I had one wish in the world, it would be to be able to read and write. The issue would be whether I could handle it. It would be *so amazing* for me, never having known that. It would be like somebody who has been born blind and there's no operation or anything anyone can do about it, and they get that one wish of being able to see. What an experience that would be for them! That's how it would be for me with reading and writing. Would that blind person be able to cope with seeing to begin with? Of course, they would adapt, but, to begin with, it would be overwhelming. Same with me and reading and writing because I've never *known* what it's like.

We had so many interviews and in one of them I said I didn't see the point, when there were some of us who couldn't even read, of going down the road about where to put capital letters and full stops – I actually knew that, anyway. That's one of the things I learned at school, although some of the others didn't. What he was teaching is beneficial for a high percentage of people who can't read and write, but it doesn't work for people who are truly dyslexic. The other dyslexic people on the course were finding it frustrating the same as me, although Jim stopped short of saying it was a waste of time.

What really upset me was that he gave me a 'B' for effort. I was driving for four hours, twice a week, and holding down a business at the same time, all of which did interfere with my earnings. That was commitment, and I put everything I had into it. To be given a 'B' was like another kick up the arse. Hey ho, it's happened all my life. He's an expert teacher, but I think he'd be man enough to admit he may not be an expert in teaching people with dyslexia; at least, I hope he would.

We actually got on really well. We're the same age and, in some ways, had the same kind of upbringing. As part of the documentary, we all went to Oxford University for a weekend to do exams. We went out the night before and had a brilliant laugh. It really was superb. Theresa, who has ten kids, had hurt her ankle that day and we managed to get a wheelchair and pushed her around the town. I think we could all say, in lots of ways, we all had a working class upbringing, but all different. Phil and I just got on so well, laughing and talking about stupid things. I think he could relate to where I'd come from and what I'd done, despite my dyslexia. We don't see eye to eye on how I should be taught – if I can ever be taught – but it was a really good evening, and laughter can conquer anything. We were all so equal that night, which was nice. We had a lot to drink and when we got back we had more to drink in the university bar. Jim and I went running the next morning, with hangovers, and then we went in to do these really tough – for us – exams. They were extremely simple to people who can read and write, in some ways embarrassingly so, but to us they were Mount Everest.

The exams were a waste of time for me, and then we found out we'd have to re-take them with an independent adjudicator for them to count. There was no way I was going to do them again. I passed two or three of them, which was good, but then on the third or fourth I was really struggling. I had a great big camera very close to my face and a little camera almost brushing my ear and I thought, *I really don't need this*. I cleared up my stuff and just walked out. They were saying, 'John, John, can we talk to you?' I told them, 'Piss off! I've had enough. Give me ten minutes or half an hour; I need to be on my own.'

I went round the corner. It was summer – a nice warm day – and I just sat down. They asked what I was feeling and the emotion came: I was cut up about it. It was just stressful and *so much* effort to do it. I'd given everything I could give to it, and it just got to me.

I could see on the others' faces how much it all meant to them. These weren't important exams for me because I've done the exams and got the qualifications I need for my work in the construction industry. For everyone's health and safety, you need City and Guilds qualifications for working on the railways and the roads and working with certain kinds of machinery. I would always ring up before a course and tell them I was dyslexic. The Equal Opportunities Act gives me the right to help, and they read the questions to me. Most people think we're thick. We're not. We're intelligent. I got 90 – 100% on the exams and the pass rate was around 70%. Every one was a big achievement for me.

More than once, I've had a boss say that dyslexia is just an excuse. When someone in the bakery trade said it to me years ago, I said, 'If you feel that that is right, I'll hand in my notice now and go where somebody doesn't think that.' He said, 'Oh no, you don't have to do that. We'll agree to disagree.' I said, 'That may be so, but I know for a fact that that's not right.' He was an intelligent guy and I think he knew he'd been a prat; there was never anything else said about it. It was just ignorance and prejudice. That's one reason I always wanted my own business: I don't have to put up with that now. Although, it still happens: only two days ago, somebody said to me, 'You use dyslexia to your advantage.' He meant it more as a joke, but would there be humour in telling a blind person that they were using blindness to their advantage? It's different, but women still have to go through that type of thing with male chauvinism. What would the word be for prejudice against dyslexics, instead of chauvinism? There isn't one; it's not recognised. But it's there.

When people are asked what dyslexia is, if they have any idea in the first place, they say it's not being able to read and write. Well, that's only the symptom. I can get through a whole day without having to read or write, but I still suffer with dyslexia every waking moment because of the thinking process. I don't think I got that over enough in the documentary. As a dyslexic being interviewed about it numerous times, I repeated myself a lot because I have a problem getting it over. In some ways, being interviewed about my dyslexia was one of the hardest things I had to do. In maybe two percent of the interviews, I felt that I really got my point of view across; ninety percent of them were bollocks! (I do love that word, 'bollocks': it's so rounded; it just 'does what it says on the tin', and it's not *too* rude! *And* I know how to spell it!)

I could see how the others in the documentary – the women, especially - were changing, and to see that confidence building in people, as I had felt it grow in myself, was priceless. It was in their faces how much it meant to them when they'd been told that they'd passed something for the first time. That was powerful. It's such a major achievement. Some of them were on benefits and one of them, Kelly, was a J K Rowling in the making - she was really good at writing, but she'd had no confidence before. They could see the world opening up in front of them. Just to be there when people are going through that journey was a good reason for doing the documentary. I didn't get much out of it, as far as reading and writing, but I've done all right in life so far and there's more to come. To see the transformation in so many of the women, though, was an honour.

Right at the end, when the filming was finishing, there was a little ceremony. One of the ladies there, Theresa, was in her late fifties, and in those six months I saw her blossom. She hadn't been taught to read and write at school. Criminal! Absolutely criminal! I don't know how it had happened. She'd gone through the school system and hadn't been given a chance. She'd never been on a bus, alone, in her life because she couldn't read; she was afraid; her confidence was 'zilch'. I saw her awaken during that course, and I got so much out of seeing her blossom. This lady was a superb mother; she had about ten kids and thirty-eight grandchildren, and she's a brilliant cook - all good, old fashioned, English cooking. She had been writing the recipes down and, for a surprise, Jill and I had a little book printed for her – about ten copies. At the end, after the teacher had done all his speeches, I got up. I'd got Jill to write down about how I'd met her and seen her blossom, and about her cooking, and I tried to read that in front of the cameras, which was a lot of pressure and I just couldn't do it. Phil tried reading it to me and me speaking it. Then he said to just say it from the heart and, as soon as he said that, it clicked, and I got out what I wanted to say. It was a magical moment that I gave to somebody who never thought that she would have a *book* of her recipes: it meant so much to her.

As far as learning to read and write in the course, I might as well have got a baseball bat and smacked myself on the arse for six months and would most probably have learned more from that! That system works for people who haven't been taught properly, and there are still a lot of people out there who haven't been taught properly, but it doesn't work for severely dyslexic people.

What I got out of the whole experience was how far I've come, despite my dyslexia, so it was good for my confidence in that way. Jim and I were the most dyslexic people there and I run my own businesses; Jim has worked hard and held down a job all his working life. I probably wouldn't have seen that five years ago; I wouldn't have been able to see the positives. The reading part disappointed me but it didn't crush me. Overall, I enjoyed it. It was a good experience in life. Not everybody gets the chance to be on a documentary. And I met superb people.

It was also a unique opportunity to get my point of view across. I hope I did, because that's what I really wanted to do. There might be somebody severely dyslexic watching it who thinks, *if he can run his own business, I can do it as well.* I had everybody telling me I couldn't; no one believed I could run my own business, but I can and I still do. I show what you can do by sheer bloody-mindedness. If I can reach the person who thinks, *yes, I can do it,* and becomes the next Richard Branson because of what I might have said or because I made something click in their brain, that would be fantastic, whether it's a man or a woman.

Women bring a lot to business. We need to see that. They bring a different angle. Jill has a different approach, and we work so well together in business, we're very fortunate. Men and women often seem to be at war with one another. If we could all work together more, a man and a woman can bring so many angles to a business table, it's brilliant. For some reason, we still seem to have some 'male chauvinist pigs' out there in business and it really annoys me. We're in the twenty first century and there are still men out there not giving women a chance. A lot of men just barge their way through and step on people's toes, and there are women who do it as well, but they always say behind a successful man there's a woman; I don't know if it works the other way!

Through Jill's eyes …

I was so excited about the documentary. At last we'd be able to reach millions of people to make them aware of what it's like to be in John's head, and other people like him, and how they're labelled and treated as lesser human beings. I felt this was something we really had to go for, even though there would be a financial backlash in that it would take up a lot of John's time.

The film crew was lovely. They made us feel so at ease, and they were so interested in us. I know they're researchers and it's part of their job, but they were so good at it: they were genuinely interested in us, and still are. It was just a really marvellous experience, probably a better one for me than it was for John. It was absolutely exhausting for him because any bookwork is exhausting for him. He really couldn't cope with the homework he was set. It was degrading for him, trying to read two-letter words again and again and again and not being able to. I was hoping for a miracle, but as soon as I knew it was phonetic I didn't think he would be able to do it, and he hasn't moved forward with it, at all. But that wasn't what the documentary was about.

It was made to uncover the truth and see the different types of people who had difficulty with reading and writing. It proved a point because the women are all reading and writing now, whereas, the dyslexic men still aren't. Phil Beadle has a real skill and a good formula for people who have fallen through the net. Maybe the women have an element of dyslexia, but phonics doesn't help John's kind of dyslexia. I liked Phil, and John really enjoyed his company, but his attitude was that he was the expert and his formula would work for anyone, eventually. Well, I'm sorry, but he's not inside my husband's head; he's not an expert on my husband's brain.

There was a party and they gave out certificates, which was a bit patronising but quite sweet, and it meant a lot to some of the others there. John runs his own business. He's on a different level. With reading and writing he's lower than them, but in intelligence, in what he's achieved in his life and what he does on a daily basis, he's far above them. He was an odd character to have on the program, but interesting for viewing.

He wanted to do a recipe book for Theresa, so I put it together and got a few copies printed. John wrote the foreword – or he told me what to write – and he wanted to read it. He stood at the lectern, with two cameras on him, and he couldn't. He couldn't read it. He knew what was in it and he'd practised it, but he couldn't read it. When Phil told him to just say it, and he started talking, he was fluent.

Phil gave him 'B' for effort and 'B' for attainment and that was a slap in the face for John. The trouble with John is that he'll look like he isn't trying. The problem is he's tried so hard he's blank, and he shrugs it off so that it looks like he can't be bothered. He just can't do it, any more than I can fly. He cannot transfer those letters into sounds. Just the other day, he asked me how to spell Halifax and, of course, I began with 'H'. He said, 'H?' I said, 'Trust me, John; it's 'H'!' And he said, 'So, where's the 'X'?' He always thought 'Halifax' began with 'X' because of the advertisement on TV; his brain couldn't make the connection with, or differentiate, the beginning and end sounds of the word.

Physically, there is a gap in his brain. Phil explained to me about the gap in the brain, and yet he still said, on camera, that with time and one to one tuition John could read. He can't. What's the point of saying he can? If he could have done, he would have done by now. Twice a week, he'd work all day, then drive two hours to get there, do the lesson and come home, grumpy, by about 9.30. After six months and all that effort, surely we would have seen some improvement if it was possible, but he got no better, at all. It made me cross that Phil couldn't see all that. Other than that, it was a fantastic experience.

Through Katy's eyes …

My dad's dyslexia has always been just something that was there; he never made a fuss about it so it was never a big issue. Even though I didn't spend a lot of time with him at first, I grew up with the fact that he's dyslexic, so it doesn't even seem weird. Even when I learned to read, I didn't find it strange that my dad couldn't; I just thought of it as *something I could do that he couldn't, in the same way that I couldn't put up signs but he could.*

The only time it felt a little bit weird was when he did the reading course for the documentary. He had a homework book and he got really frustrated with it because he couldn't do it. Even to me, some of it seemed pointless, but that's probably because I take it for granted that I can read. It was connecting letters to sounds and was quite weird and confusing. He was never in a very good mood when he was doing it and I was trying to teach him, which felt strange. They were asking how he saw words - to try and explain his dyslexia - and that felt strange, too, because I never really saw it like that; it was just something that he had.

That's the only point in my life, ever, when it's felt strained and even awkward with my dad. I don't really even know why, except that it's the one part of him that I don't understand, at all. Part of me doesn't like that because he's my dad, but Jill will say, too, 'Do you have any idea what's going on inside your dad's head?' because she doesn't and I don't. It's not something that troubles me, I just think the reading course made me realise I have no clue what my dad goes through, every day, because I only see the outside; I don't see what's happening on the inside, and he doesn't talk about how hard he finds things. It was really difficult for me to watch him reading, getting things wrong and getting frustrated. I'd never seen him struggle with that before because if he couldn't do something he would ask, and although he wasn't learning anything by that, it was easier for me to see. Watching him struggle to do something that I could do in two seconds was horrible.

Beforehand, you wouldn't be surprised if someone told you he was dyslexic, but now he's so much more confident and, speaking to him about everyday things, I think you would be surprised. It's only when he's talking about something he finds really hard, like reading and writing, that you understand more, but you can never understand completely. The thing that makes me really angry is when people use it against him, because he's not lazy; it's not his choice not to be able to read and write properly. I feel very protective of him over things like that; maybe more than I should be, because he can easily stick up for himself now.

Sometimes he'll say he can't do something because he's dyslexic and Jill will say, 'Don't label yourself like that. How about you just try?' I find that quite funny because he can't do those things, but he will find his own funny way around them. He might be reading something and it all looks quite normal, but I know he's not really reading it: he'll take ten times longer than I would, for a start, and probably won't get half of the words right, but he might get the main gist of it. But I don't think about it because he'll ask for help if he needs it; he's not embarrassed or anything. He's just my dad. I can't imagine him any other way.

For part of the documentary, I want back to Charles Dickens, my old school, and spent a day there. They did this with a couple of us because I don't think they knew what else to do with us. It was the first time I'd really gone back. There are plans to redevelop it and make it into a really modern school of the twenty first century, with a dome and everything. I went round all the old classes, talked about the way they do things now and the way we did it then; I saw the resources they have today compared to what they had in my day, and it was all completely different. There are still children falling through the net, but I wouldn't think that's happening at Charles Dickens now.

I thought it would be weird, going back, but I hadn't thought about how. I was treated like a VIP, which is ironic since it was the reverse when I was at the school. There's a lovely head teacher there now and you could see he loved that school and wanted to make it better. And that's how it should be because they have young people's lives in their hands, and those lives can be crushed

I walked into the hall and saw myself sitting there over twenty-five years ago, in an exam, not being able to read any of the questions. I didn't really let a lot of my feelings out during that documentary, but all that was on camera: I was standing there and I could feel the demons leaving me. It was like being cleansed. It was almost a spiritual experience. I think a lot of people need to do that, but I think the schools would have to have a full-time person to be able to take all the ex-pupils round!

I'm not staying bitter about it because you get more and more bitter and end up a twisted wreck; I won't allow my life to be like that. Yes, there were a few nasty teachers, who told me to go on the dole for the rest of my life because I wouldn't make anything of it, and some of them had no time for me, at all; they failed me - no doubt about that - but most of them did try. I *have* to believe that. There was a time I was extremely bitter about it all, but I've had to change the way I look back at it to be able to live how I want. They had to push me out of the way because I needed so much time: I needed one to one. I can't change the past, but I can change my future. Over the last five years, with counselling, and counselling myself to change my attitude for the best, that bitterness had to go or I could not have moved on to make my life and my future how I want it. So, for my own sake, I try to see the best in those teachers, or else I'd be stuck in the past. It's here and now that's important, not what happened thirty-five years ago. It can stay in the past.

To have the opportunity of going back and getting rid of those demons that had haunted me for years was something else the documentary gave me. Now they're gone. I left them there, and I know they'll be ripped down with the old part of the school. It's lovely. It wouldn't actually matter if it wasn't ripped down but it's poignant and symbolic. With it being rebuilt, it's one of the best schools in Thanet now. It was the worst when I was there, but we did have a good rugby team!

CHOICE

Belief in yourself is spiritual. Religion is good, but self-belief is where change happens. There are still times when I look back at myself, especially since I've been doing the book, and I think, *was it just a dream*? I know there's no way I can go back; it's like two completely different people.

The way I am now has become the norm but, every so often, something makes it clear, like seeing the sun shining on autumn leaves or feeling it on my back. We were at a rugby game the other Sunday and it was cold, but the sun was out and for the first time in quite a while it was beating on my back. It felt warm, and that was *nice*. My feet were cold because it was icy on the grass, but the sun was on the back of my head and my neck for about half an hour and that was *good*. And it was free! Nature gives you that. Just this morning we had our personal trainer come in for us to do our training session at home, and afterwards we were having a cup of tea in the lounge. I was looking out of the window at the frost on the car, and as the sun came round the house it was melting the frost. It was absolutely beautiful the way the warmth went across the car, and melted droplets ran down the side. That's just *there* to enjoy. How many people would even notice it? I would have missed all that, before, because I was so wrapped up in myself.

If you're given things like that, which are free, how can you fail to be happy. You have to choose to be unhappy for that not to make you happy: it is as simple as that. And I chose unhappiness for myself up until five years ago: it was my choice. There were lots of different reasons, some of them my fault, some of them other people's fault, and some of them just the way things are but, with hindsight, I can see that it was a choice to be unhappy. I focused on the miserable parts instead of the happy parts because of one thing - dyslexia. The crux of the matter was that I was dyslexic, and I made myself miserable. I still am dyslexic, but I'm happy. It's choice.

Jill's mum was telling her that Desmond Tutu (I'd love to meet him.) said if someone has had turmoil in their life and they write about it, it cleanses them so that they're almost born again in the spiritual sense. And it has done that for me. I've been so comfortable in the last five years without the depression I used to have, it's hitting home to me more and more that I have to move on to be the businessman I can be and want to be.

I have a good friend who runs a little business called 'Wordzrock'. She sells small stones with sayings on them; they can be funny or spiritual; they can be for somebody's birthday, christening, marriage and so on. I got her to do one for me saying, *All I need is within me now.* And I carry that with me all the time. It's an anchor so that, every time I put my hand in my pocket and touch it, I remember to use those tools to keep me moving on with what I need. I can't read it, but I know what it says. I need to move on again and it's exciting but frightening at the same time. I'm growing; I'm not just standing still. The book has closed a chapter of my life and an exciting new chapter is opening up. I feel that emotionally, mentally and physically.

EPILOGUE

For five years I stayed in that comfort zone of really liking where I am. After years of depression, it just felt *so* good, drifting along in that lovely, lovely bubble. And it was scary to break out of it. But now, I'm out on a limb again.

In those five years, I listened to books about the law of attraction, which I would have said was a load of bollocks before. But seeing how my life changed after I changed my attitude and, without realising it at first, looked at the positive side of things, I know it works. Whatever you put out to whatever you want to call it - the Universe, God or your inner self – does come back, and I'm proof of that.

Now, I'm tired of not having enough money behind me to move things on to where I want them to be, so I'm concentrating on that. The one key thing missing from my life is financial wealth, but I *feel* that it's there for me and I'm attracting it: I get more cheques through the post than ever before, and I've asked for the paperwork on some new units being built near where I live. I've got a lovely, glossy picture of what they're going to look like and I've put that over my computer so that I can see it, because, within a year, I want to move my business into one of them and I'm visualising being in it.

I'm doing a lot more for myself, too, rather than waiting for somebody else to do it for me. I wanted brochures for my UVShield company, and I didn't think I could do them. I asked a couple of people to help me, but we're all busy and in the end I just got pissed off waiting. I signed up to a website called 'Best Of Deal and Sandwich'. They're all over the country but that's my area. Loads of different companies advertise on the site, they get a lot of hits, and my window film company comes near the top on Google. When I was signing up, they had a chat with me about my company and what I'd done, and they'd written all the text for me, for the site. So, for the brochure, I took a lot off that with my reading software, put pictures in, Jill laid it out for me, and I took it to the printers and got it done.

Doing that would be nothing to a lot of people but, to me, it was huge. It was scary, but bloody exciting, as well. Being so dyslexic and putting a brochure together was massive for me. The brochure isn't perfect, and I put it off and put if off because I wanted it to be exactly right, but you have to strike a balance and do what you can do.

I actually found a spelling mistake on my website. It was only an 'r' that was missing off 'your', but I saw it and heard it, as well. I do try to follow the written words along with the software and, in that instant, I recognised the word. I might look at it later and not recognise it again, but, in that instant, I did, and it was a very nice moment.

I didn't think I'd ever know anything about what Google would pick up, and key words, and search engine spiders! But I have my own website now and Jill and I have been working on it, putting in key words and putting on more pictures of jobs I've done instead of using stock photos from the Internet. Very generally, I know how my website needs to work to get the most out of it. It's easier for me, now, because of my reading software, but it still took a lot of belief in myself to get a website up and running. It's worth knowing about my competitors too, although there are still some sites that the software can't read. And actually, it doesn't matter how many competitors I have: you just make yourself the best you can be.

I also took a course on window film, which I found on the Internet by finding the right key words to put in. (It's the same with my brain: if I put in the right key words, the right thing comes out!) There is no actual qualification in window film at the moment, although that is changing, but I decided a course was a good thing to do, and it's the way the government thinks these days, too. And though I already knew how to do it, I learned such a lot because it was one to one tuition and the guy who taught me had done that type of work for years. He showed me all kinds of tips and how to get round the wrinkles. It was worth ten times the £320 I paid because of the confidence it's given me to know I can go in and do a top rate job. I was almost there before, but I needed all those little tips.

I've got a good resource now, too, because they're on the other end of the phone if I need installers for a big job. I also found out where to find a certain kind of cutter, which I'd been looking for but couldn't source - they sell them and I bought one! And there's another course I can go on when I've got a unit and want to start working on cars - window tinting and that type of thing - plus there's a lot of computer software to learn. So it's a business that I'm finding a challenge, and I haven't had a challenge in business for a good few years.

Some people prefer to stick with what's easy, but I'm now one of those people who has to keep on growing inside. To do that, you have to keep stretching yourself and stretching yourself as a human being. Just because I've got dyslexia doesn't mean I can't move myself into something I thought I never ever could. I know that there's so much more in me to give and I can stretch to anywhere now. I believe in myself and I'm attracting wealth and the way I want to be. I've only reached a small percent of my potential, so far. I now believe I can have the business that, because of my dyslexia, I always thought was just a dream.

Joining Breakfast Networking International six months ago was a big leap for me. I put more in than I was getting out of it to begin with, but that's starting to work for me because I'm getting to know people, and that's where I heard about the 'Best Of' site. When I first joined, I didn't know if I'd be able to keep up with them, but it's the law of attraction working again: I've met my peers, the people I'm like and want to be like, because I don't put myself down in my own mind anymore. I'm attracting more and more successful people into my life and they're getting to know me.

I'm not the best talker during my sixty seconds of explaining what I do: every week it's slightly different because of how my brain works, so some weeks it's better than others. Most people would probably say that, but there's fear in standing up and talking to a group of people, and to be able to conquer that, with my degree of dyslexia, shows an amazing transformation. I'm living my dream and that's *fucking amazing!*

I said, earlier in the book, about having streams of income that make money for you even when you're asleep. One good way is on e-bay, and I've always wanted an e-bay business. I've still got a few things to learn about it, but I put a shop on there with the friend who has the 'Wordzrock' business. Everybody wants to be an e-bay millionaire. I don't know if I'll do that with the rocks, but it could be very good for us, financially.

E-bay is the written word again and it's a big challenge because e-bay is not very well set up for people with disabilities, and I'm not saying that's their fault, because the set-up works really well. And as the site has been developed, I've noticed over the past year or two that my software is finding it easier to pick up and read what's on there. But, even with the software, it's a still big challenge for someone who can't read and write. I have to keep pushing myself, and I do find ways around it by putting things in a separate document, where the software can read it. It takes a lot longer, but I enjoy it because I feel I'm achieving something. I really believe I can get over the hurdles, so I'm going for it. What an amazing achievement that would be: a severe dyslexic with an e-bay business doing really well. That would be the ultimate, because I want to show that I can use my mind for success as well as my hands. I want to show that there's intelligence in people with severe dyslexia: we're not slow and thick.

To get the law of attraction working for you, you have to keep moving on and believing in *you*. I go to networking evenings now that even six months ago I didn't feel, in myself, that I could do. At the end of the day, it's just talking to people and listening. You've got two ears and one mouth: use them, in that order - your ears twice as often as your mouth! Always listen first, instead of trying to force yourself on people. Then they're a lot more willing to listen to you. When you're nervous, you can let your mouth run away with you. Every time I'm going up to somebody to ask what they do and tell them what I do, and, in my mind, I'm pulling the string up on my head to get more oxygen into my brain, I remind myself of that: two ears, one mouth; listen twice as much as you talk. It works for me.

Doing this book has cleansed me: baggage has been unpacked and put away; demons have been slain and laid to rest; the world is off my shoulders and I feel lighter. I felt the world had been lifted from me when I had the awakening too. It's different this time because I know that in another five years, three months, three weeks or five minutes there are going to be other challenges, and I'm going to metamorphosise into something new; it'll be like another awakening.

Nothing will be nicer than seeing the name of my company above the door of a unit again, and sponsoring Dover Rugby Club in the big way that I want to, knowing that the money is there to do that: not for the glory, but to give back. That's very important.

You have to take everything you can out of life because the better you feel about yourself, the more you give back. It becomes infectious in the end, which I think would be quite nice for the world. The majority of people just exist; a small minority *live*. Shouldn't that be the other way round?

MIND TOOLS

Choice.

Follow your bliss.

Believe the good things, not the bad.

All you need is within you.

'Whether you think you can or you think you can't, you're probably right.'
- Henry Ford

'If you believe life will be a baggy load of nut sacks, it will be!'
- John Tipping

It's all down to thought.

Step back and be open to thought.

What you think is a boulder in your path may only be a pebble.

The piece of string.

The two arrows.

When would 'now' be a good time?